The Literary Persona

The
Literary
Persona

Robert C. Elliott

The University of Chicago Press
Chicago and London

Robert C. Elliott taught at the University of California at San Diego from 1946 until his death in 1981. Among his books are *The Power of Satire* (1960) and *The Shape of Utopia* (1970).

The University of Chicago Press, Chicago 60637
The University of Chicago Press, Ltd., London

Library of Congress Cataloging in Publication Data

Elliott, Robert C., 1914–81
   The literary persona.

   Includes index.
   1. Persona (Literature)   2. Criticism.
3. Swift, Jonathan, 1667–1745—Criticism and interpretation.   I. Title.
PN218.E48   801'.95   81-19656
ISBN 0-226-20502-9   AACR2

Contents

Foreword

Robert Elliott died suddenly on April 13, 1981, while hiking on a favorite trail in the Palm Canyon at Borrego Springs, California. He was sixty-six years old and evidently in excellent health. Certainly he was active and vigorous to the last: younger in appearance than his years, always at the forefront of the intellectual territory he so enjoyed exploring, still a demon on the squash court, a hard-working (and hard-worked) colleague, and—as always—a much cherished friend of many persons of all ages.

Not long before his death he completed this book, the fruit of many years of research, meditation, and experience: its richness derives from all three of these elements, framed by a fine lucid intelligence and a rare grace of expression. It is possible, now that he is dead, to discern in Robert Elliott's scholarly production a developing and now completed pattern. In *The Power of Satire* (1960) and *The Shape of Utopia* (1970) there is an obvious connection, for satire inevitably entails consideration of utopia; both depend crucially on the representation of disguises of the self that is the subject of the present book. All deal with man in the world, the choices he can make, and those which are forced upon him. Robert Elliott was a man of action, and his works bear witness not to a belief in mankind's perfectibility but to a determination to clarify, and thus make the world more tolerable.

ANDREW WRIGHT

Preface

The term *persona* has a long literary history going back to classical drama; but over the last two generations the word has become associated with a way of interpreting literary texts that can only be called revolutionary. It is no longer possible to read the work of Chaucer or Thomas More or Jonathan Swift or Alexander Pope—or indeed that of Horace or Juvenal, or even Dante, or that of Proust or a hundred other contemporary writers—as it was read before the word *persona* entered the critical vocabulary. Revolutions, needless to say, are never peaceful, and many people loathe the term (which has, in truth, been abused to the point where its usefulness is in question) and the kind of criticism with which it is associated. Most recently, Robert Wilson, who has published in *Critical Inquiry* and other respectable places, characterizes *persona* as a thoroughly execrable term, conceptually empty and pretentious. Why, Mr. Wilson wonders, do critics whore after it? This book is an attempt to answer that question—or if not exactly that question, one much like it phrased in somewhat more decorous language.[1]

1. Wilson's comments, along with many of a similar kind, appear in a long dialogue between him and the Australian writer Vincent Buckley, who, al-

To put it as simply as I can: the word *persona* is used by literary interpreters in an effort to clarify the relationship between the writer—the historical person—and the characters the writer creates. That relationship is never simple—Flaubert's "Madame Bovary, c'est moi" legislates complexity—but it is made more difficult when the writer uses the first person singular pronoun, when he writes "I." The situation becomes even more tangled when the writer identifies himself (or somebody with his name, or part of his name) as a character in his poem or fiction: Chaucer in *The Canterbury Tales* and many of his other works, Thomas More in *Utopia,* Proust in *A la recherche du temps perdu,* Borges and Christopher Isherwood in their tales. The history of confusions arising from these rhetorical situations is vast. I believe that the doctrine of the persona was introduced into critical discourse in an effort to cope with some of the most exigent difficulties. In this book, which deals primarily with the writer's use of the first person pronoun, I shall try to sort out some of the problems attendant on that effort.

Part one of the book deals with the concept of the literary persona in historical terms. The first chapter traces the introduction of the term *persona* into critical discourse and looks at some arguments among scholars over the word and kind of criticism associated with it. Chapter two sketches the history of the term itself from its original sense of *mask* in Latin through its semantic development—a development of extraordinary complexity and interest—into our words *person, personality,* French *personne,* and various cognate terms. Part two takes up certain theoretical questions lying at the heart of the controversy over persona criticism, particularly as these questions bear on the writer's use of the first person pronoun. How "sincere" are the autobiographical poems of Alexander Pope or Wordsworth, the con-

though more temperate, also attacks the term and the critical position associated with it. "Persona: the Empty Mask," *Quadrant* (Australia) 19 (November 1975): 82, 92. The chief target of Wilson and Buckley is George T. Wright in his "The Faces of the Poet," the first chapter of his book *The Poet in the Poem* (Berkeley, University of California Press, 1960). In my view this is a brilliant essay, the best thing ever written on the *persona.* I am much indebted to it.

fessional poems of Robert Lowell? What is the status of sincerity as a literary criterion? What truth claims are involved in a work of fiction written in the first person: Proust's work, for example, Christopher Isherwood's, Norman Mailer's? To what degree and in what sense is the poet's "true" self implicated in the "I" of his poems? Large questions these, and small prospects of satisfactory answers; but some hopes, perhaps, of clarifying issues.

Part three of the book consists of three essays examining Jonathan Swift's use of the first person pronoun in his prose and his poetry: Swift's "I." The choice of Swift is arbitrary, although all the issues associated with use of the first person are present in his work, and it would be hard to think of a writer who deploys the "I" with more skill or greater intricacy. In any event for me the choice was inevitable: my concern with the persona issue stems directly from my many years' engagement with Swift's writing. As long ago as the early 1950s the concept of the persona made it possible for me to make a kind of sense, I thought (no matter how crude a sense), of the structure of Swift's *Tale of a Tub,* something I had not succeeded in accomplishing without that enabling concept. It provided in addition a way of looking at a number of kinds of literature over and beyond the literature of irony; and many people, of course, shared my sense of its value. Thus when in the 1960s and later the idea of the persona came under attack from distinguished critics—Irvin Ehrenpreis, Bertrand Bronson, Donald Davie, Lionel Trilling—I was prompted to look more closely into the aesthetic issues at stake. The first two parts of this book are the result of that examination; the third is an attempt to test out on Swift's work the principles of persona criticism.

From a theoretical point of view influential today this whole enterprise must seem anachronistic. Structuralist and poststructuralist theory in France and the United States attempts to abolish the notion of the self as conscious subject altogether. To write about an author's "I" as though it had some kind of substantial existence is to write about an illusion: the self is a construct, constituted entirely by a variety of social and linguistic codes of which it is a mere function. Man in this view has been displaced as a center or source of creativity. This new wave from France—this French Connection, as Geoffrey Hartman calls it—powerful and disturbing in its implications, is founded on philosophical assumptions about language and the relation of language to reality radically different from my own more traditional assumptions. Thus although some of the writers of this newest New Criticism and I may have a subject in common— the writer's "I"—there is no true engagement of ideas: the two discourses do not meet.[2]

Another disclaimer: when I have presented earlier versions of some of this material before audiences a response has sometimes been, Why didn't you talk about Browning's use of the persona, or Diderot's, or John Barth's? My answer has had to be that Browning or Diderot or Barth—or any of countless other writers—would have fitted admirably into the discussion. My choice of examples again is arbitrary, limited by many factors not least of which is ignorance. This is a small book on a very large subject.

2. See Jonathan Culler, *Structuralist Poetics* (Ithaca: Cornell University Press, 1975), 28ff. and throughout; Denis Donoghue, *The Sovereign Ghost* (Berkeley: University of California Press, 1976), 38ff.; Murray Krieger, *Poetic Presence and Illusion* (Baltimore: Johns Hopkins University Press, 1979), esp. 139–87.

Acknowledgments

To all of the people and certain institutions who have helped me in various ways to bring this book to completion, I wish to express my gratitude.

I am indebted to the National Endowment for the Humanities, whose Fellowship supported my work for the year 1979–80, and to the Committee on Research at the University of California, San Diego, which provided funds for research and the typing of the finished manuscript.

My thanks to the staff members of the Widener Library at Harvard University and the London Library and, especially, to the library staff at the University of California, San Diego, who have been consistently helpful to me.

In the preparation of my manuscript, I was fortunate to have the assistance of Martha Robinson, who expertly and patiently transformed my sometimes all but illegible handwriting into perfectly typed pages. June Vayo, in the summer of 1979, served me well as research assistant. As for my graduate students, I hope they realize how much I value the creative role they play in my work.

The numerous friends and colleagues who read part or all of the manuscript as it progressed were generous in their attention and suggestions; and I want, especially, to thank Frederick S. Bailey, Morton W. Bloomfield, Page duBois, Stephen Gilman, Don Wayne, and Kurt Wolff. In particular, I am deeply grateful to Robert I. Levy for the careful critical reading he gave my work: he brought to bear upon it a rare sensitivity to the issue of the *persona,* and the suggestions he made have been of inestimable value to me. My appreciation of Roy Harvey Pearce, colleague/friend of all these years, goes almost without saying: he stood by as always—concerned, critical, encouraging.

Much more than thanks, again and ever, to Mary, who believes much more in people than in masks.

Part 1

The
Literary
Persona

History

> "A *persona* is the invoked
> being of the muse; a siren audible
> through a lifetime's wax in the ears;
> a translation of what we did not
> know that we knew ourselves:
> what we partly are."
>
> R. P. Blackmur, "The Language
> of Silence"

1 The Embattled Persona

Writing many years before *persona* became a popular critical term, but reacting to the same stimulus which later brought it into favor, George Lyman Kittredge produced a splendid example of so-called persona criticism without using the word. In his chapter on *The Book of the Duchess* in *Chaucer and his Poetry* (1915) Kittredge writes eloquently of the quality of artlessness and naïveté which contributes so much charm to the poem. He is nearly as eloquent in expressing his contempt for the many critics who confuse the "artlessness" of the poem with Chaucer's artlessness, its naïveté with his. "A naïf Collector of Customs," says Kittredge, "would be a paradoxical monster." *The Book of the Duchess,* we recall, is a dream-vision, recounted in the first person by the Dreamer, who is innocence itself. But because the Dreamer speaks in the first person, critics identified him with Geoffrey Chaucer: Chaucer dreamed a dream and characterizes himself in the telling of it. This, says Kittredge, is nonsense: the Dreamer "is a purely imaginary figure, to whom certain purely imaginary things happen, in a purely imaginary dream. He is as much a part of the fiction in the Book of the Duchess as the Merchant or the Pardoner or the Host is a part of the fiction in the Canterbury Tales."[1]

1. George Lyman Kittredge, *Chaucer and His Poetry,* Introduction by B. J. Whiting (Cambridge, Mass.: Harvard University Press, 1970; orig. pub. 1915), 45–48.

3

This critical insight—commonplace today although still contested—was to have momentous consequences in Chaucer criticism. It is interesting that although he edges up to the issue Kittredge does not apply the same kind of analysis to the *Canterbury Tales*. The Canterbury Pilgrimage, he writes, is "a Human Comedy, and the Knight and the Miller and the Pardoner and the Wife of Bath and the rest [which must include the pilgrim who recounts the whole affair] are the *dramatis personae.*" A few pages later he reiterates: the Pilgrimage is not painting or delineation but dramatic action. Thus Chaucer "makes himself one of the Pilgrims, in order that we may understand that they are as real as he is." Because Chaucer existed, our reasoning goes, his companions on the pilgrimage must have existed in the same way: an effective maneuver in the interests of realism. But of course on another level the obverse holds: if the Pilgrims are as real as Chaucer, he, in the poem, is as unreal as they—or as the Dreamer in the *Book of the Duchess*. Kittredge does not push the logic of his earlier analysis this far, but there can be no doubt that he was interested in such ontological oddities. Near the end of the dream in the *Book of the Duchess* the mournful Knight finally tells the Dreamer the source of his sorrow: his lady is dead. The Dreamer responds: "Is that your los? By God, it is routhe." The two ride together back to the castle. A bell in the castle strikes twelve. The Dreamer awakes. "Was it a real sound this time?" asks Kittredge, toying with the relationship among the purely imaginary Dreamer, the imaginary world of his dreams, and the flesh-and-blood Geoffrey Chaucer, who also had dreams.[2]

Later critics, as we shall see, adapted Kittredge's way of distinguishing between the narrative "I" and Chaucer by using the term *persona;* but before looking at that development I want to refer to another great scholar who analyzed brilliantly a number of examples of the split between narrator-"I" and author in

2. Kittredge, 154–55, 161, 53. Had Kittredge thought of the narrator of the *Canterbury Tales* as a fictional character on a plane with the Wife of Bath and the Pardoner, and hence the agent of the author's irony, it is unlikely that he would have accepted so wholeheartedly the narrator's entirely positive evaluation of the charming Prioress.

medieval literature without using the word *persona*. Leo Spitzer maintains that in the Middle Ages there was a widely accepted distinction between what he calls the "poetic I" and the "empirical I." The concept of literary property hardly existed; the audience understood that in writing "I" the poet represented not himself in a personal way, but himself insofar as he represented mankind. Although the common people of Ravenna may have looked with awe on Dante as a man who had actually journeyed through Hell and Purgatory to Paradise, more sophisticated readers of the poem would have understood that Dante's "poetic 'I' represented . . . the human soul as such with all its capacity to attain to the Beyond and to reach out of space toward its Creator." At the same time, says Spitzer, Dante the narrator, as opposed to Dante the protagonist, included many factual details about his personal life, not because he was interested in himself as himself (as later Petrarch and Montaigne were to be interested in themselves), but because both aspects of the "I," the poetic and the empirical, were necessary; "on the one hand, he must transcend the limitations of individuality in order to gain an experience of universal experience; on the other, an individual eye is necessary to perceive and to fix the matter of experience."[3]

Other medieval works, problematic because of their first person mode of telling and the consequent embroilment in issues of biographical fact and responsibility, lend themselves to interpretation by Spitzer's method. For example, the long fourteenth-century Spanish poem *Libro de Buen Amor,* composed by Juan Ruiz, Archpriest of Hita. A work of lovely charm and formidable heterogeneity, the *Libro de Buen Amor* is given what unity it has by the fact that the Archpriest is at once author (doubtless also oral performer), narrator, and protagonist. He represents himself as taking part in many episodes, some of them of decidedly unpriestly character. A constant narrative thread, for example, concerns his involvement with the bawd Trotaconventos (Convent-trotter) and the sexual affairs she

<hr>

3. Leo Spitzer, "Note on the Poetic and the Empirical 'I' in Medieval Authors," *Traditio* 4 (1946): 416.

promotes for him; and some of the best-known episodes of the poem have to do with Rabelaisian encounters between the narrator, the "I," and several lusty mountain women. In short, Juan Ruiz, Archpriest of Hita, by writing in the first person and identifying himself as the protagonist (he is often addressed as "Archpriest") interjects himself into biographical and aesthetic issues of great complexity. Is the Archpriest, the inevitable question goes, writing about actual occurrences? To what degree is he incriminating himself in the sexual embroilments he recounts with such gusto? Spitzer says that through the agency of the "poetic I" the incrimination is not at the level of biographical fact but at the level of the Archpriest's recognition of his own complicity in the human condition. Although he repeatedly describes himself as participating in the episodes, he reveals himself, says Spitzer, "not as having committed the sins he describes, but as capable, in his human weakness, of having committed them."[4]

América Castro claims that it would be childish to argue over whether the "I" of the poem is or is not Juan Ruiz; although every line "gives the impression of personality, of a unique person talking," the voice we hear is not to be identified with the historical "I" of the poet. Childish or no, the argument continues; all agree, however, that the relation between the "I" of the *Libro de Buen Amor* and the Archpriest of Hita is higly ambiguous and that to take the assertions of the speaker as applying directly to the author is dangerous indeed.[5]

4. Spitzer, 418–22. The *yo* of the poem undergoes startling transformations. At one point (stanza 70) he identifies himself with his own book and virtually makes the reader the true creator: "I, this book, am akin to all instruments of music: according as you point [play music] well or badly, so, most assuredly, will I speak" (trans. Raymond S. Willis; see next note). At other points (stanzas 727, 873) the *yo* becomes momentarily Don Melón de la Huerta. My thanks to Stephen Gilman for his help with this poem.

5. América Castro, *The Structure of Spanish History*, trans. Edmund L. King (Princeton: Princeton University Press, 1954), 392, 394. That the "I" of the poem is not entirely poetic is established by some of the biographical details Ruiz includes. In the poem the Archpriest brags that he wrote many songs for Jews, Moors, students—this in violation of ecclesiastical regulations. Some of the songs survive. See Maria Rosa Lida de Malkiel, *Two Spanish Masterpieces: the*

The same cautions should be exercised, Spitzer maintains, in interpreting even so apparently confessional a work as Villon's *Grand Testament:* although established facts of Villon's life may accord with matters narrated in the artistic work, it is not legitimate, he says, to treat the materials from life and the materials from literature as interchangeable. Nowhere in this important article does Spitzer use the word *persona,* which in the applicable sense had not at the time of writing (1946) achieved wide currency, but his procedure is that of the interpreters who today use the concept of the persona in the most sensitive way.[6]

Spitzer's example, by the way, and there are many others, is enough to do away with Robert Wilson's curious contention that whereas a new class of experience ordinarily entails the introduction of a new word, *persona* was introduced into the lexicon of criticism accompanied by claims that it created a new experience, the new term preceding the experience it purports to reveal.[7]

To return now briefly to Chaucer criticism: although Kittredge's insistence on separating the "I" of the Dreamer from the "I" of Geoffrey Chaucer in the *Book of the Duchess* caused and still causes heated comment, scholars at the time of publication were immersed in antiquarian preoccupations, and not until after the Second World War, with the increasing interest in formal problems in literature, was his insight picked up by critics who were prepared to use it effectively. Talbot Donaldson's highly influential essay "Chaucer the Pilgrim" (1954) brought to bear on the structure of the *Canterbury Tales* a mode of analysis very like that of Kittredge. Donaldson distinguishes between Chaucer the pilgrim, the wide-eyed, observant, but essentially

---

Book of Good Love and the Celestina, University of Illinois Studies in Language and Literature 49 (Urbana: University of Illinois, 1961), 10. For a careful analysis of the biographical issues and an account of the scholarship, see Anthony N. Zahareas, *The Art of Juan Ruiz, Archpriest of Hita* (Madrid: Estudios de Literatura Española, 1965). An excellent text, English paraphrase, and commentary may be found in the edition of the *Libro* by Raymond S. Willis (Princeton: Princeton University Press, 1972).

6. Spitzer, 419.
7. Wilson, "Persona: the Empty Mask," 82.

uncomprehending character to whom the Host condescends, and whom the Man of Law treats as though he were not there—between that character and Chaucer the sophisticated poet. The pilgrim, narrator of the entire work, may resemble his creator in many respects; still, says Donaldson, he is "the victim of the poet's pervasive—not merely sporadic—irony. And as such he is also the chief agent by which the poet achieves his wonderfully complex, ironic, comic, serious vision of a world." According to Donaldson, the pilgrim belongs to the ancient, honored, and much misunderstood tradition of the fallible first person singular; his closest counterpart is Lemuel Gulliver.[8]

In the early 1950s, when "Chaucer the Pilgrim" was published, the literary public had been sensitized by the popularity of Henry James and the hegemony of the New Criticism to irony and its issues, to matters of authorial point of view, and indeed to questions about the fallible first person singular. As a way of dealing with these matters the word *persona* had been picked up, an indirect result, it seems likely, of use by Ezra Pound. Pound called an early volume of his poems, published in England, *Personae* (1919); then when his collected poems were published in the United States in 1926, he used the same title. *Personae* was reprinted in this country a number of times through the 1940s and 50s. Pound commented on the title in an essay he wrote entitled "Vorticism," which he later included in the volume he wrote on his friend the sculptor Gaudier-Brzeska (1916; reissued 1939):

> In the "search for oneself," in the search for "sincere self-expression," one gropes, one finds some seeming verity. One says "I am" this, that, or the other, and with the words scarcely uttered one ceases to be that thing.
>
> I began this search for the real in a book called *Personae,* casting off, as it were, complete masks of the self in each poem.

8. E. Talbot Donaldson, "Chaucer the Pilgrim," *PMLA* 69 (1954); reprinted in Donaldson, *Speaking of Chaucer* (London: Athlone Press, 1970), 3, 8.

During these same years Yeats wrote often of masks, for him (in his private terminology) the very source of creative energy, and Carl Jung used the words *persona* and *mask* as central terms in his psychoanalytic theories.

Given this authoritative stimulus and given also what was becoming an obsessive preoccupation of the age with questions about the self, it is not surprising that by the late 1940s the word *persona* had entered definitively into the language of critical discourse.

Thus Talbot Donaldson in the essay previously referred to speaks of Chaucer's using the device of the persona in order "to present a vision of the social world imposed on one of the moral world." The description of the pilgrims by one of themselves, one who is identified as the recounter of the tales but who is shown to be remarkably insensitive to the import of what he recounts—this makes, says Donaldson, for a moral realism even greater than the literary realism for which Chaucer is so widely celebrated. It provides a double vision in which the realistic and the moral are perfectly fused.[9]

By proposing a new way to look at the *Canterbury Tales,* Donaldson's essay injected new life into Chaucer criticism, stimulated many papers, some of them following his line of approach, some modifying it, a substantial number coming out in flat opposition. From the beginning the whole idea of the persona has been abhorrent to certain critics: this "schizoid notion of two Chaucers," Bertrand Bronson, a powerful voice for the negative, characterizes it. Nine-tenths of the talk about Chaucer's persona, Bronson claims, is palpably mistaken: if, instead of looking at Chaucer in the poem, we look at a substitute "existing as an independent fiction in a cast of characters," we destroy the ironic game of which Chaucer was master; we break the personal, teasing, highly nuanced bond between him and his audience. The idea of the persona comes, Bronson maintains, from the post-Gutenberg world; it has no

9. Donaldson, 9.

applicability to the world in which Chaucer lived. Bronson's strictures, directed principally at Donaldson, although he is not named, have been quoted repeatedly in the literature of Chaucer criticism, and the issues he raises are being urgently debated today.[10]

From the historical perspective of the 1980s it hardly seems surprising that at about the time Donaldson's essay appeared (priority is not an issue) Dante scholars were applying a similar mode of analysis (in effect, an elaboration of Spitzer's insight) to the *Commedia*. Francis Fergusson, writing in the early 1950s, insisted that "the distinction between Dante speaking as the author, and Dante the Pilgrim, is fundamental to the whole structure" of the poem. The Pilgrim is the protagonist of a drama: whereas the author knows the whole story in advance, the Pilgrim encounters each episode freshly, in innocence, the two perspectives providing a kind of stereoptical effect. Out of the tensions generated here arise the complex movement of the poem and its suspense. John Freccero speaks of the Augustinian *present* which gave Dante a place to stand and from which he could see himself in time past, a present spanning "the necessary gap between the being of his *persona* and the knowing of the poet." In recent years a major theme of Dante criticism has been the attempt to work out the implications of the distinction between Dante the author and the persona he created—the Pilgrim who makes his way through Hell and Purgatory to Paradise, from ignorance to knowledge.[11]

10. For an account (up to 1968) of the controversy prompted by Donaldson's essay, see Dieter Mehl, "Erscheinungsformen des Erzählers in Chaucers 'Canterbury Tales,'" in *Chaucer und seine Zeit,* ed. Arno Esch (Tübingen: Niemeyer, 1968); Bertrand H. Bronson, *In Search of Chaucer* (Toronto: University of Toronto Press, 1960), 25–33.

11. Francis Fergusson, *Dante's Drama of the Mind* (Princeton: Princeton University Press, 1953), 9–10. John Freccero, Introduction to his edition of *Dante: a Collection of Critical Essays* (Englewood Cliffs, N.J.: Prentice-Hall, 1965), 4–7. For an account of the major work employing this or a similar interpretative approach in Dante studies, see Lawrence Baldassaro, "Dante the Pilgrim: Everyman as Sinner," *Dante Studies* 92 (1974): 63–76. Paul G. Ruggiers, *The Art of the Canterbury Tales* (Madison: University of Wisconsin Press, 1965), 16ff., compares Chaucer's use of the persona with Dante's.

Eighteenth-century studies had its analogue to Donaldson's "Chaucer the Pilgrim" in Maynard Mack's "The Muse of Satire" (1951), which preceded Donaldson's paper by a couple of years and has proved one of the most influential essays of its kind published since World War II—influential not only for the study of Alexander Pope's satire specifically (the essay centers on the *Epistle to Dr. Arbuthnot*) but for the study of satire as a genre. Mack's approach to Pope's *Arbuthnot* was, again, not unprecedented. In 1939 Elder Olson, reacting to the notorious confusion between poetic value and the personality of Alexander Pope, analyzed the *Epistle to Dr. Arbuthnot* as an example of rhetoric on the ground that satire and didactic are overtly concerned with influencing an audience and are structured accordingly. From this point of view the poet's presentation of himself in the poem, as in *Arbuthnot,* has rhetorical but no particular biographical significance; that is, it is a main concern of the poet, in the poem, to convince his readers that he is a man of good character, thus to increase his credibility and, as a consequence, his ability to influence his audience. Whether the poet is in fact a man of good character or not is (to Aristotelians at any rate, if not to followers of Quintilian) beside the point. Thus the "Pope" of the *Epistle to Dr. Arbuthnot* (and by extension all first person projections of the satirist, whoever he might be) had no necessary relation in the moral or biographical sphere to the Alexander Pope who wrote the poem. To approach satire as rhetoric was in effect to banish the poet from the poem.[12]

Ricardo Quintana in a strong article on Swift's satirical method also stressed the impersonality of satire, its rhetorical character; he speaks of Swift's putting on a personality, a nonself "who spoke and therefore thought a new idiom," of the creative freedom this alter ego brought Swift. Maynard Mack, however, provided the essential formulation (and, incidentally, gave academic respectability to the word *persona* used in a critical

12. Maynard Mack, "The Muse of Satire," *Yale Review* 41 (1951): 80–92; frequently reprinted, e.g., in *Satire: Modern Essays in Criticism,* ed. Ronald Paulson (Englewood Cliffs, N.J.: Prentice-Hall, 1971). Elder Olson, "Rhetoric and the Appreciation of Pope," *Modern Philology* 37 (1939–40): 13–35.

context). I still remember the thrill of discovery his essay "The Muse of Satire" gave to me; and to judge from the way its echoes have reverberated in the field many others must have experienced a similar response. Emphasizing the artifice of satire, its strong element of fictionality, Mack distinguishes the major "voices" that Pope created for himself in his formal satires. The "Pope" of the poems, so self-serving, so unpleasantly hypocritical in the view of nineteenth-century critics ("If wrong, I smiled; if right, I kissed the rod"—this from one of the most combative poets who ever wrote), came to be seen as a partially artificial construct, attached in the most dubious ways to Alexander Pope of Twickenham. Of the first person speaker in Pope's satires Mack writes: "We may call this speaker Pope, if we wish, but only if we remember that he always reveals himself as a character in a drama, not as a man confiding in us." When Wordsworth writes, "to be young was very heaven," his *young* is authenticated by the facts of his life; when Pope writes "forgive the Prejudice of Youth," he is fifty. Pope's youth, says Mack, "is true only of the satiric speaker of the poem, who is an assumed identity, a persona." Mack goes on to delineate three principal voices associated with that persona: that of the *vir bonus,* the *ingénu,* and the hero. We have heard much of those voices since.[13]

To "split" Pope in these ways and in effect to assign him different selves was congenial to a period which, as I say, was almost obsessively concerned with problems of identity, the nature of the self, and role playing. "It is probably no mere historical accident," says Robert E. Park, the sociologist, "that the word person, in its first meaning, is a mask. It is rather a recognition of the fact that everyone is always and everywhere, more or less consciously, playing a rôle. . . . It is in these rôles that we know each other; it is in these rôles that we know ourselves." Given this approach to the self, it seemed fully reasonable that

---

13. Ricardo Quintana, "Situational Satire: A Commentary on the Method of Swift," *University of Toronto Quarterly* 17 (1947–48): 135. Mack, "Muse of Satire," 80–92.

the "I" of the poet represented in any given context should be
taken as only one of many possible masks that he might assume.
To what degree the mask is equivalent to the true person—
or whether "true person" has any meaning in this context—is
unresolved.[14]

The essays of Olson, Quintana, Mack, Fergusson, Donaldson
were, of course, only part of a massive shift in literary opinion
that had been going on since the early years of the century—
a shift away from nineteenth-century orthodoxies and center-
ing on the proposition that literature is, or ought to be,
impersonal—as far as possible from the confessional style of
much nineteenth-century writing. So widespread was agreement on this notion that it brought into alliance the most unlikely figures: T. S. Eliot, who identified the progress of an artist
with the extinction of personality, and Jean-Paul Sartre, who
urged that novels should be written as though they were natural
events rather than the products of man, as though they had
no authors at all. The New Critics and their followers programmatically excluded from their enterprise, as outside the
purview of true artistic interest, information about the authors
of poems, their personalities and intentions, these exclusions
facilitating exploration at new depths into the ambiguities of
poetic language and the complexities of literary structure. Gains
made here were very great indeed. On the other hand, the inevitable costs associated with the sometimes arbitrary renunciations mounted over the years, and it is now clear that the
movement has run its course as critics and readers decry the
formalism of the past generation, and authors flaunt personality
in their war against the incipient facelessness of our time. (The
recent importation of even more stringent formalisms from
France raises questions beyond the scope of this essay.) The
reaction against impersonality has been as strong in eighteenth-
century studies as in the literary world at large. How can we
possibly hope to understand a writer's art and mind apart from

14. Robert E. Park, *Race and Culture* (Glencoe, Ill.: Free Press, 1950), 249–50.

his personality, asks John Traugott. Where but from his personality does his art come? So, whereas the introduction into eighteenth-century studies of the rhetorical approach to certain classes of literary work was immensely stimulating, that approach itself is now under heavy attack. James Clifford said that the argument over these matters is one of the most significant developments in eighteenth-century studies in recent times.[15]

The debate has been strongly focused in a controversy over the role of the persona in satire initiated by Irvin Ehrenpreis, the distinguished Swift scholar and critic of contemporary poetry, whose essay "Personae" in the festschrift for A. D. McKillop (1963) appeared with something of a thunderclap. Despite a few kind words, Ehrenpreis regards the concept of the persona when used as a critical tool as at best an unfortunate mistake. In his view when we characterize the "I" of the *Epistle to Dr. Arbuthnot* as a persona, we imply a complete remove between the sentiments expressed by the "I" and those of Pope himself. By this interpretative method we effectively remove Pope from the poem. Interested critics, says Ehrenpreis, have used the persona as a device to insulate writers from their own meanings: violent or distasteful expressions in the work of Pope or Swift can be attributed to the persona, this bit of casuistry serving to protect the integrity of the author and the impersonality of the work. "To the degree that the speaker in the *Epistle to Dr. Arbuthnot* does not stand for Alexander Pope, no man, in a single speech, can be wholly himself." Ehrenpreis recommends that instead of talking about the masks and personae of literary satire we deal with the satirist directly, recognizing that his impersonations of folly point, however obliquely, to what the author truly means and is.[16]

The reaction to Ehrenpreis's essay has been extraordinary. A

15. James L. Clifford, "The Eighteenth Century," *Modern Language Quarterly* 26 (1965): 120ff.

16. Irvin Ehrenpreis, "Personae," in *Restoration and Eighteenth-Century Literature: Studies in Honor of A. D. McKillop,* ed. Carroll Camden (Chicago: University of Chicago Press, 1963), 28; reprinted in Ehrenpreis, *Literary Meaning and Augustan Values* (Charlottesville: University Press of Virginia, 1974), 51.

symposium on its thesis in the *Satire Newsletter* (Spring 1966) had eighteen participants, sixty-four pages of debate. Numerous references to the article have appeared in the journals, and it has been the focus of many sessions in seminars and at professional meetings. Clearly a good deal of pent-up feeling had accumulated around the persona issue; Ehrenpreis opened a vent. Much of the response that has poured forth has taken something of this form: Thank God that in talking about *A Tale of A Tub* (or *Arbuthnot* or whatever) we no longer have to speak of the Hack or the puppet or the persona or the mask—or even of the Tale-teller—but can come right out and say Jonathan Swift. The joy in unloading formalisms, which in Swift studies has sometimes reached Byzantine complexity, has been manifest. Despite such attacks, however, the idea of the persona continues to be widely used in eighteenth-century studies, although the word itself is employed perhaps more sparingly and with greater caution than was evident thirty years ago.

Not long before his death Gilbert Highet, the famous classical scholar, issued a blast against the introduction of the persona into critical parlance, his animus directed chiefly against those who brought the idea of the persona to bear on the satires of Juvenal and Horace. Highet's principal targets are William S. Anderson, a classical scholar who had analyzed the satirical masks of Juvenal, particularly differentiating the "I" of the satires from their author, and Alvin Kernan, to whose theory of satire (which is based on a concept of the persona), developed in his powerful and important book *The Cankered Muse* (1959), Anderson gratefully acknowledges his debt. The persona theory will not work, says Highet; almost inevitably it distorts the work of the poets to which it is applied. When Horace inveighs against adultery in his satires, he is sincere, he means what he says; and the fact that in *Satires* 2.7 his slave Davus accuses him of being a wife-chaser indicates simply that Horace has been unable to live up to his principles. Persona critics, says Highet, make the "I" of the satires into nothing more than a ventriloquist's dummy, a complete misjudgment of the actual situation: "it is not the fictitious and ineffective 'tensions' of a satirical

persona that we see in Horace's satires, but the ethical contradictions of a real man." As with Horace, so with Lucilius and
Boileau and Pope and Byron. Highet's disapproval of the
method (which, to be sure, undermines his own mode of criticism) is very strong indeed.[17]

Criticism of the older literatures often lags a few years behind,
in method and in theoretical orientation, what preoccupies contemporary writers and those who write about them. It is not
hard to see the trickle-down process operating from the "little"
magazines and the advanced critical journals to *PMLA*. In the
"modernist" literature of the first half of the twentieth century
the idea of the persona is everywhere. Popularized by Ezra
Pound, given impetus by Yeats, institutionalized by Eliot in his
poetry and his criticism, the notion of the persona is at the center
of that phase of modernism which holds that the "I" of a poem
is always a dramatized "I," no more to be identified with the
actual poet living in history than the Bishop ordering his tomb
is to be identified with Robert Browning. Pound's comment
on Mauberley and Prufrock holds for most literary "I's" of the
period: "(Of course I'm no more Mauberley than Eliot is Prufrock. Mais passons.) Mauberley is a mere surface." To identify
"I" and author was as illegitimate as to inquire into authorial
"sincerity," a dim practice of nineteenth-century critics that
seemed finally laid to rest. Poets and New Critics were de-
termined to avoid what Henry James called "the lyric leak."[18]
    It was a shock to such convictions when in the 1950s the
"confessional" poetry of Robert Lowell, Allen Ginsberg, and
their colleagues in the United States and Great Britain—the most

17. Gilbert Highet, "Masks and Faces in Satire," *Hermes: Zeitschrift für Klas-
sische Philologie* 102 (1974): 321–37; William S. Anderson, "The Roman Socrates:
Horace and His Satires," in *Satire: Critical Essays on Roman Literature,* ed. J. P.
Sullivan (Bloomington: Indiana University Press, 1968) and *Anger in Juvenal and
Seneca,* University of California Publications in Classical Philology, 19 (Berke-
ley: University of California, 1964), 127–96.
    18. Ezra Pound to Felix Schilling, July 1922, in *Letters, 1907–41,* ed. D. D.
Paige (New York: New Directions, 1971), 180.

powerful poetry of its time—seemed to demand an entirely new (or very old) approach to the poet's "I." Lowell wrote about himself in *Life Studies* (1959) in unmistakably autobiographical terms, the "I" of the poems expressing facts, feelings, ideas torn from the turbulent life experience of the poet. Ginsberg's *Howl!* was his own howl at his times. In the view of certain notable critics—Donald Davie, Lionel Trilling—these extraordinary developments in poetry have effectively scuttled the doctrine of the persona (a contention that we will examine in chapter three) at least insofar as it applies to poetry after the eighteenth century. Instead of thinking of the "I" as a mask, we are in for a period of identifying "I" and author, say these critics, a period in which "sincerity" becomes once again a criterion of poetic value. It is a development, says Mr. Davie, that we should welcome, and perhaps we should, although I think no one can look forward with pleasure to articles in *PMLA* on Chaucer's naïveté.[19]

In this rapid survey of the fortunes of the persona as applied to literary interpretation, definitions have been lacking and the grounds for the controversies which seem inevitably to accompany introduction of the concept into virgin literary territory have been brushed over lightly. The persona is a vigorously contested concept; although it seems to have established itself fairly securely in critical discourse (always excepting structuralist and poststructuralist discourse), strong opponents urge against it strong arguments. It is clear, if only from the heat generated by the arguments, that the issues involved go far beyond simple matters of critical method. They are deep and fundamental: at stake, if not always overtly, are questions about the nature of the self, about sincerity and its values, about the truth claims of literature—unavoidable issues if we want to understand why persona criticism has had such a powerful impact and why it is contested so sharply.

Before turning to these issues, however, some clarification is

19. Donald Davie, "On Sincerity: from Wordsworth to Ginsberg," *Encounter,* October 1968, 61–66; Lionel Trilling, *Sincerity and Authenticity* (Cambridge, Mass.: Harvard University Press, 1972), 6–10.

in order. Anyone looking seriously at the controversies over the persona quickly sees that much argument is terminological rather than substantive. Opponents are not agreed on what their central term means. Writers who attack the persona are likely to think the term entails a complete separation between the author and the pose he assumes: the mask having nothing to do with the wearer of the mask. Proponents have a much more flexible idea of the relation between persona and author, mask and wearer becoming almost indistinguishable at times. Given the history of the terms, such disagreements are hardly surprising. *Persona* has one of the most complex histories known to philologists, a history full of contradiction, controversy, enigma. Sober German philologists have been known to go into raptures over the obscure provenance and tangled permutations of the word. No one is certain even of its origin. A famous American psychologist devoted a long chapter in a major book on psychology to tracing the history of the term: from *persona,* of course, come our *person, personality,* and other cognates. Gordon Allport identifies fifty different meanings of the word and its cognates and arranges those meanings schematically in a series of diagrams showing the historical development of each meaning and its relation to all the others. I do not know what historical linguists may think of Allport's schematic diagrams, but they seem to me a remarkable achievement in historical semantic analysis. As I trace the development of some of the important meanings of *persona* in the sketch that follows, I shall be following Allport as well as more professional philologists.[20]

20. Gordon W. Allport, *Personality: a Psychological Interpretation* (New York: Henry Holt, 1937), 25–50.

2 The Word
Persona

"Rational beings are designated 'persons' [*Personen*]," wrote Kant, "because their nature indicates that they are ends in themselves." It is one of the great curiosities in the history of the language that our word *person*, in Latin *persona*, meaning the mask an actor wore on the stage, should become for Kant the term incorporating the moral essence of human beings; the concepts behind *person* and *personality* constitute the foundation on which his entire ethical system is constructed.[1]

Latin usage is illustrated by this brief fable from Phaedrus:

> Personam tragicam forte vulpus viderat:
> "O quanta species" inquit "cerebrum non habet!"

[A fox, after looking by chance at a tragic actor's mask, remarked: "O what a majestic face is here, but it has no brains!"]

The etymology of *persona* has long been a vexed question and there is no certainty in the matter yet. Some scholars, reaching far, have tried to derive the word from *prosôpon*, Greek for *mask*. Aullus Gellius proposed that it came from *personando* (sounding

1. Immanuel Kant, *Foundations of the Metaphysics of Morals* in *Critique of Practical Reason and Other Writings in Moral Philosophy*, trans. and ed. Lewis White Beck (Chicago: University of Chicago Press, 1949), 86–87; and see the *Critique of Practical Reason*, 193.

through) on the theory that the mask provided a kind of megaphone effect for the actor's voice. Sir Arthur Pickard-Cambridge among others disposes of the theory as well as the derivation. In the Renaissance, Julius Caesar Scaliger proposed a derivation from *peri sôma* (around the body), and scholars have resuscitated a good many other more or less remote suggestions. Hans Rheinfelder in a 200-page monograph on the word has a full account of these and other etymological speculations. Until recently the most widely accepted derivation (accepted by J. B. Greenough and G. L. Kittredge in *Words and Their Ways in English Speech,* 1928, and favored by the *OED*) has linked *persona* with *personāre* (to sound through) although, as the *OED* points out, the long *o* in *persona* is a difficulty.[2]

Today, a very different derivation is accepted by most (but not all) authorities. In the Tomb of the Augurs in Tarquinii, Etruria, dating from about the sixth century B.C., there is depicted on one of the walls a pre-Roman gladiatorial combat. One combatant swings a club, but ineffectively, for his head is covered by a sack or a cloth, obscuring his vision, and his legs are entangled in a long leash. At one end of the leash is a fierce dog which is attacking him. The dog is being urged on by a bearded man wearing a peaked cap and a mask. An inscription identifies the masked man as Phersu. In another painting the masked figure (again identified as Phersu) is shown running away from something. Most philologists now derive *persona,* the Latin name for a theatrical mask, from the masked Etruscan gladiator, Phersu. This derivation has at least the advantage of placing the emphasis on the visual aspect of the mask rather than on its alleged acoustic properties.[3]

Whatever the uncertainties about derivation, there is no ques-

2. Phaedrus, bk. 1, fable 7, in *Babrius and Phaedrus,* trans. and ed. Ben Edwin Perry, Loeb Library (Cambridge: Harvard University Press, 1965), 201. Sir Arthur Pickard-Cambridge, *The Dramatic Festivals of Athens,* 2d ed., rev. J. Gould and D. M. Lewis (Oxford: Oxford University Press, 1968), 195–96. Hans Rheinfelder, *Das Wort 'Persona,'* Beihefte zur Zeitschrift für Romanische Philologie, 77 (Halle: Niemeyer, 1928).

3. See Alois Walde, *Lateinisches Etymologisches Wörterbuch,* new edition by J. B. Hofmann (Heidelberg: Carl Winter, Universitätsverlag, 1954); cf. A. Ernout and

tion that, in Latin, *persona* refers originally to a device of transformation and concealment on the theatrical stage. That over the years this word becomes, as Adolf Trendelenburg puts it in Kantian terms, the expression of the moral essence in man, of that which is most characteristic of man, is surely a development to wonder at. On second thought, however, perhaps not: the question of what it is to be a person—a *real* person, as we say—has always had its enigmatic aspects; and masks are mysterious things.[4]

From the beginning of recorded history, and far back beyond that in cultural time, people have donned masks in the service of various transformative activities—for purposes of entertainment, certainly, including "play-acting"—but also in their efforts to communicate with the spirits and with their gods, even to partake of godhood. Ethnologists have collected a massive assortment of materials about the ceremonial use of masks all over the world. What Raymond D. Fogelson says of the transcendent importance of masks to the North American Iroquois is true of many other people. When an Iroquois puts on the mask, says Fogelson, he is not impersonating the False Face spirit; instead he *becomes* the spirit, he is assimilated into the being of the spirit, a phenomenon of participation of a kind that the French philosopher Lucien Lévy-Bruhl described many years ago. Thus among the Iroquois (and many others) to don the mask in the appropriate ceremonial circumstances and settings is not to enact a role, to make believe, but temporarily to incarnate cosmic reality. Clearly this reverses our normal categories: instead of the mask as a bogus front, hiding the real person behind it, for the Iroquois and the others the mask mediates the highest reality of all.[5]

A. Meillet, *Dictionnaire étymologique de la langue latine*, 4th ed. (Paris: Librairie C. Klincksieck, 1967). For the tomb paintings see Luisa Banti, *Etruscan Cities and Their Culture*, trans. Erika Bizzarri (Berkeley: University of California Press, 1973), 75–77; William Beare, *The Roman Stage*, 3d ed. (London: Methuen, 1964), 22.

4. Adolf Trendelenburg, "A Contribution to the History of the Word Person: a Posthumous Treatise," trans. Carl H. Haessler, *The Monist* 20 (1910): 336–63.

5. Raymond D. Fogelson, "The Anthropology of the Self," unpublished

The use of masks in ancient Greek and Roman drama quite possibly developed out of roughly comparable modes of belief, immensely different as the societies in question certainly are. According to uncertain tradition, Thespis, who is said to have introduced tragedy to Athens, at first disguised his face with white lead and only and only later took to wearing linen masks on the stage. Aeschylus was the first to use colored masks with terrifying features. Behind these dramatic performances, however, were the more "primitive" activities from which the drama evolved: the religious festivals honoring the god Dionysus, festivals characterized by the frenzied dancing of worshipers masked as satyrs and maenads. Masking was an essential element in the worship of many gods in Greece. Even so conservative a scholar as Pickard-Cambridge acknowledges that to put on the mask of the god meant that the worshiper was taking on something of the god's potency—the structural similarity here with the experience of many remote people, separated by vast stretches of time, is unmistakable. In the Dionysiac revels, masks were worn perhaps in part, Pickard-Cambridge suggests, to protect the identities of respectable citizens in the goings-on which became very disreputable indeed, but principally, he affirms, to make possible "the strong sense of 'identification'" with the god that the mask provided.[6]

Roman drama too developed out of roughly comparable celebrations, out of the "Fescennine jesting," the metrical exchanges of obscenity and taunt that sound like the phallic songs Aristotle identifies as the source of Athenian comedy. In the *Georgics* (2.380ff.) Virgil says that the Athenians sacrificed a goat to Dionysus on the day that dramatic performances took place and, amidst much revelry, the winning poets were crowned. Similarly, he says, the Latins had their bacchanalian wine festivals at which they covered their faces with hideous masks made of bark, improvised wild verses, and hung sacred images of Bac-

---

paper, presented to a conference on "New Approaches to the Self" at the Center for Psychological Studies in 1979.

6. Pickard-Cambridge, *Dramatic Festivals*, 191.

chus in the trees. Strong as Etruscan and Greek influences are on early Roman theater, it seems likely that the originating germs of the drama and the use of masks therein are to be found in the masked revelry of the harvest festival as Virgil describes it.[7]

When over the course of time the forms of dance and ritual celebration became crystallized into the structures of drama as we know it in its earliest stages, masks, naturally enough, were retained. Their function now, however, would be very different as the drama becomes secularized, a long remove from the magicoreligious participation in the being of the god. As a secular device used by actors playing deliberately conceived roles, the mask becomes available for a wide variety of social uses, and the Latin word for *mask* experiences a kind of semantic explosion. One segment of the explosion gives us our word *person* and the immense complex of ideas surrounding it.[8]

No doubt it is impossible to write the history of this development in any factual sense. Marcel Mauss, the distinguished French anthropologist, in an attempt to show how we have arrived at our own Western notion of *person*, makes the Roman transformation of the concept of *persona* crucial: "Ce sont les Romains qui ont transformé la notion de masque, personnalité mythique, en notion de personne morale [the social person]. . . . Le fait était grand et nouveau." Like his uncle Emile Durkheim, Mauss believed that notions of the self among primitive people are relatively undifferentiated, bound up with roles in ritual observance, with the magicoreligious significance of names— the product, in short, of socially ordained institutions and influences. This view, that the *personne morale* is in some sense

---

7. Beare, *Roman Stage*, chap. 2, "The Italian Origins of Latin Drama," 10–23.

8. The process is in certain respects analogous to that in which "magical" satire with its power to kill is desacralized and can then evolve into the literary forms we know. See Robert C. Elliott, *The Power of Satire: Magic, Ritual, Art* (Princeton: Princeton University Press, 1960), 87–99. Some elements of the mythical identification may linger in the United States even today. When a court order forbade an aging Clayton Moore to wear the mask of the Lone Ranger as he had worn it in public appearances for many years, Moore responded: "When I put on the mask I become the Lone Ranger." *Boston Globe*, September 4, 1979, p. 1.

created and defined by society, has had enormous influence on anthropologists, psychologists, sociologists. "I would maintain," writes the anthropologist Meyer Fortes, "that the notion of the person in the Maussian sense is intrinsic to the very nature and structure of human society and human social behaviour everywhere."[9]

Mauss believed that the ancient Greeks, Etruscans, Latins lived in an ambience of primitive belief, their notions of self consonant with what Cassirer called mythically bound consciousness. The Romans took the crucial step. In the Huxley Memorial Lecture before the Royal Anthropological Institute (1938) Mauss says that perhaps the step was not taken immediately.

> I imagine that legends such as that of the consul Brutus and his son, of the end of the right of the *pater* to kill his own sons, his *sui,* convey the acquisition of the *persona* by the sons, even during their father's lifetime. I think that the revolt of the plebs, the full civil rights acquired—after the sons of senatorial families—by all the plebeian members of the *gentes,* was decisive. All the free men of Rome became Roman citizens, all acquired the civil *persona;* some became religious *personae;* some masks, names and rituals remained linked to a few privileged families of the religious *collegia.*

Thus, whereas a great many societies have arrived at the notion of personhood *(personnage)* as a role in the sacred dramas of the tribe, in Rome, says Mauss, "the 'person' is more than an organizational fact, more than a name or a right to a role and a ritual mask; it is a fundamental fact of law." Once desacralized, *persona* gets caught up in the evolution of Roman law, an essential step in the achievement of our Western idea of the person as

---

9. Marcel Mauss, "Mentalité archaïque et catégories de pensée," in *Oeuvres* (Paris: Editions de Minuit, 1969), 2:132. Meyer Fortes, "On the Concept of the Person among the Tallensi," in *La Notion de Personne en Afrique Noire,* Colloques Internationaux du Centre National de la Recherche Scientifique, No. 544 (Paris: Editions C.N.R.S., 1973), 288.

an independent entity. The mask, which was originally a mythic representation, comes to signify a social personality.[10]

Mauss's historical speculations are attractive and can serve, provisionally, as a model, although one can grant to them no more than a kind of aesthetic validity: there is, of course, no history for much of the material he deals with. Instead, myths, traditions, stories—many stories. For example, it is said that Roscius, the great Roman actor, the friend of Cicero, introduced the mask to the Roman stage as a matter of personal vanity: he wanted to hide his squint. (This reminds me of an amusing "commonsense" explanation of a strange phenomenon in Irish mythology: it is said that in order to acquire occult knowledge the great hero Finn chewed on his thumb. The explanation: Finn had the habit of biting his nails.) Roscius' squint will hardly do to account for a phenomenon that goes deep into the Latin cultural past; and as for dates there is ample evidence (although it is contested) that masks were worn on the stage in the time of Plautus and Terence and that in their time the word *persona* was taking on new meanings. From the simple "false face" worn by an actor the word carries the meaning in Terence of the *role* played by an actor: *agit personam* (he plays a part) and even the applied sense of specific characters in drama, as in Terence's acknowledgment that he got some of his characters (*personas*) from Greek plays.[11]

The term rapidly took on a further assortment of associated meanings to the point where in the writings of a single author a number of distinct significations of *persona* can be distinguished. Cicero, as Trendelenburg, Max Müller, and others have pointed out, is an excellent example. When he writes to Atticus: "Quid

---

10. Marcel Mauss, "Une catégorie de l'esprit humaine: la notion de personne, celle de 'moi,'" *Journal of the Royal Anthropological Institute* 68 (1938): 275, 274; English translation by Ben Brewster in Mauss, *Sociology and Psychology: Essays* (London: Routledge and Kegan Paul, 1979), 80, 78. Cf. Jean Duvignand, "The Theatre in Society: Society in the Theatre," in *Sociology of Literature and Drama,* ed. Elizabeth and Tom Burns (Harmondsworth: Penguin, 1973), 95.

11. Terence, *The Eunuch,* 1.32. For full discussion of this controversial matter see Beare, Appendix I, 303–9.

est autem, cur ego personatus ambulem?" (Why should I wear a
mask [or assume a character] before men's eyes?), *personatus* has
to do with false appearance, a meaning close to the original sense
of mask. "Is not old age itself a mask [*persona*] ugly enough?"
Cicero goes on to ask. (Unlike *persona,* the adjectival form *personatus* retained its restricted meaning of deliberate counterfeit,
as in our *personate.*) Seneca writes "Non hominibus tantum, sed
rebus persona demenda est et reddenda facies sua" (We should
strip the mask, not only from men, but from things, and restore
to each object its own aspect).[12]

Another transformation of the word, one vitally important in
the history of thought, refers not to the mask nor to the dramatic
character represented by the mask, but to the actor himself as an
individual; and from there to any individual: his real nature and
personal (it is hard to avoid the term) character. Cicero writes to
Julius Caesar: "et ad eam rationem existimabam satis aptam esse
et naturam et personam meam" (and for that purpose I considered my own character and personal qualities very suitable).[13]

At one point, reflecting on his political past, Cicero writes that
his *persona* has always been such as to invite the attacks of the
wicked: here the meaning is clearly that of role in life rather than
in drama. The word appears in a similar sense in legal discourse
as roles are assigned to plaintiff, defendant, and judge. Cicero's
consciousness of the different, possibly conflicting, roles one
plays in life and in law has a distinctly twentieth-century ring;
the following statement would be at home in a sociology
textbook. Cicero says that he makes a practice of arguing the
opponent's case to his own client; then, when the client has left
and he is alone "with perfect impartiality I play three characters
(or roles) [*tres personas*], myself, my opponent, and the arbi-

12. Cicero, *Letters to Atticus,* XV, 1, trans. E. O. Winstedt (Cambridge: Harvard University Press, Loeb, 1953), 3:294–95. Seneca, *Ad Lucilium Epistolae
Morales,* XXIV, 13, trans. Richard M. Gummere (Cambridge: Harvard University Press, Loeb, 1953), 1:172–73.
13. *Letters to Atticus,* IX, 11a; cited by F. Max Müller, *Biographies of Words*
(London: Longmans, Green and Co., 1888), 39.

trator." Cicero sounds as though he has been seeing Pirandello on the Roman stage.[14]

Still another meaning found in Cicero associates *persona* with rank and dignity, as in our *personage*. Allport sums up the distinct meanings of the term found in Cicero's writing thus:

a) as one appears to others (but not as one really is);
b) the part someone (*e.g.*, a philosopher) plays in life;
c) an assemblage of personal qualities that fit a man for his work;
d) distinction and dignity (as in a style of writing).[15]

In early Roman law persons have rights, things have none: *persona* is set off against *res* and *personae* includes all human beings. By the time of Justinian, however, it is established that slaves have no rights in law, and indeed slaves are not persons: *servos quasi nec personam habentes* (slaves [are regarded] as having no persons)—slaves are things. (Our twentieth-century equivalents are the "nonpersons" of political victimization.) Christian moralists refused to accept the dehumanizing of slaves and went on to make a metaphysical entity of the person. The word itself became embroiled in the fierce conflicts in the early days of Christianity over the terminology most appropriate to designate the nature of the Trinity. Tertullian and the Western church in general used *persona,* with its sense of roles, to specify the threefold nature of God; the Greek church argued for *hypostasis* (substance or essential nature). Gregory of Nazianus finally made a reconciliation possible, and the controversy of the Trinitarians and the Monophysites was officially brought to a close by the finding of the Nicaean Council (A.D. 325): *Unitas in tres personas, una persona in duas naturas.* Over the centuries, however, this divine mystery proved to be a solution that was the source of endless conflict. One of the heresies of which Servetus was convicted, after the accusation by Calvin in the sixteenth

14. Cicero, *De Oratore,* II, xxiv, 102, trans. E. W. Sutton, completed by Horace Rackham (Cambridge: Harvard University Press, Loeb, 1948), 275.
15. Allport, *Personality,* 26.

century, was that he had underhandedly distorted the meaning of *persona* in his *De trinitatis erroribus* (1532). Servetus was burned at the stake. In December 1979 the Reverend Edward Schillebeeckx, a Professor of Theology at Catholic University in Nijmegen, the Netherlands, was called before the Sacred Congregation for the Doctrine of the Faith (formerly the Holy Office) at the Vatican, where he was interrogated on matters of dogma. In an interview Father Schillebeeckx spoke of the difficulty of interpreting the dogma proclaimed by the Council of Chalcedon (A.D. 451) which upheld the Nicaean doctrine, defining the nature of Jesus as being both true God and true man. Father Schillebeeckx accepts the dogma but finds a semantic difficulty because "the word 'person' in the fifth century had a different meaning from today."[16]

Apart from such complications *persona* became one of the most honorific terms in the lexicons of theology and philosophy: for Aquinas "a person means that which is most perfect in nature." Centuries earlier Boethius had provided a crucial definition: "Persona est substantia individua rationalis naturae (Person is the indivisible [individual] substance of a rational nature), thus linking personality with the rational life and making possible the gradual enhancement of the individual as a unique, self-conscious being, a development culminating in Kant and the Romantics.[17]

In our day the term is still at the heart of some of our most intransigent philosophical, theological, ethical problems. Philosophers, trying to determine what constitutes a person, debate the mind-body problem. We—the lay public—become philosophers, theologians, moralists as we participate in the urgent political controversy surrounding the issue of abortion, which turns on the meaning of *person*. "When is a person a person?" asks an Anglican minister in anguished tones, and on the answer incalculable results depend.[18]

16. Trendelenburg, 348–56; cf. Mauss in his Huxley Lecture, 278–79. For Schillebeeckx see the *New York Times*, December 16, 1979, p. 3.

17. Cited and translated by Erich Frank, *Philosophical Understanding and Religious Truth* (Oxford: Oxford University Press, 1945), 176.

18. *Los Angeles Times*, August 27, 1978, part 5, p. 5.

The original association of *persona* with the stage made the word available not only for mysteries like that of the Trinity but for some of the more primitive mysteries of grammar. The ancient Greeks, probably the Stoics who founded modern grammar, gave the word *prosopon* (mask) to the inflectional endings of the verb, and the Romans, translating *prosopon,* followed their usage; thus we speak of the "person" of the verb. According to Trendelenburg, the Greeks must have had in mind the drama where persons really move as "I" and "you." The character on the stage who speaks is called the first "mask," perhaps, suggests Trendelenburg, because he initiates dialogue. He is an "I"; he speaks, as we say, in the first person. (Trendelenburg suggests a psychological explanation for the nomenclature according to which "the 'I' is called the first person because to everyone the 'I' is first and closest.") The first "mask" speaks to a second "mask": you, thou; he speaks, that is, in the first person to a second person. (According to James Harris, an eighteenth-century philosopher of rhetoric, the "authors of language" reasoned that because the person addressed is "next in dignity to the Speaker, or at least comes next with reference to the discourse," they called the pronoun that of the second part or person.) The "mask" spoken of is the third person. Following Greek example, Varro, the great Roman rhetorician, puts the whole matter succinctly: "cum item personarum natura triplex esset, qui loqueretur, [ad quem], de quo" (the persons of the verb were likewise of three natures, the one who was speaking, the one to whom the speaking was done, and the one about whom the speaking took place).[19]

Such matter-of-fact formulations, however, do not remove all the drama or the mysteries of dialogue even when looked at under the aspect of the grammatical. The first persona speaks to the second—the "I" to "you"—then suddenly roles are reversed as the "you" becomes an "I" and the "I" "you." As speech

19. Trendelenburg, 349. James Harris, *Hermes: or a Philosophical Inquiry Concerning Language and Universal Grammar* (London, 1751; reprinted by Scolar Press, 1968), 64–67. Varro, *On the Latin Language,* VIII, 20, trans. Roland G. Kent, (Cambridge: Harvard University Press, Loeb, 1958), 2:387.

passes to the lips of the third in dignity, former "I's" and "you's" become "he's" and "she's" while the former "he" is elevated to "I." Rainer Werner Fassbinder plays cleverly with these complexities, which are handled so effortlessly by competent speakers of a language, in his film *The Marriage of Maria Braun*. A black American soldier is teaching Maria English: "This is a tree," and she repeats "This is a tree"; "That is a bird," and she repeats "That is a bird." "I am a black man and you are a white woman." She repeats: "I am a black man and you are a white woman." The intricate game between personae breaks down as rules are violated—a source of comedy for characters and audience alike.

In the first person grammatical category there are depths and perplexities of an endlessly alluring kind. How extraordinary it is that "I" somehow encompasses in a coherent way the thousand and one selves that constitute a "Self," and that the person whom one loves and the person one loathes also say "I." Ian Michael, a historian of grammar blessed with style and wit, writes this:

> It is easy to regard the first person as more than a grammatical category: it seems to contain the speaker's conception of himself as being distinct from other people. Accordingly, the speaker's name, so closely involved in his awareness of his own identity, would seem to "have" something of this quality of person. Again, the movement of the verb in *He sees me* can be regarded not only as (in some sense) an action, but also as a movement of person. The coiling utterance of the speaker moves round person after person. It starts from the speaker, an "I"; it embraces another person, a "he"; it returns to the speaker. The verb is related on the one hand to the "he," on the other to the "me"; it somehow mediates the change of person.

The instabilities of the grammatical person were voluminously debated over the centuries. Apollonius, Roger Bacon, many others consider whether there might be more than three persons, or whether a verb might be impersonal, or how the relation of person to verbs, pronouns, and nouns differs. *Person* "kept much of its human reference," says Michael, "and never fully became a neutral technical term: its metaphor was still active."[20]

Given the enormous spectrum of meanings taken on over the centuries by the word *persona* and its cognates, any generalization about the term must be suspect—any generalization except this one: the most striking characteristic of the term is its polysemous nature, the contradictory range of its reference. In French, *personne* signifies both somebody, a person, and in certain usages, nobody. My friend Denise Sigaud tells me of a colleague of hers, a foundling in infancy, who was given the name Personne: he is known as M. Personne. A personage is someone of high importance. "Who is *that* person?" can imply contempt. For C. G. Jung the persona is "only a mask of the collective psyche.... Fundamentally the persona is nothing real." Kant, on the other hand, constructs his whole system of ethical thought on the foundation of his concept of person and personality. Personality frees man "from the mechanism of nature," writes Kant; it "elevates man above himself as a part of the world of sense"; in it is the root and origin of duty. As against this lofty concept consider twentieth-century usage: "She is a Hollywood (or TV) personality"—here the word signifies a spectacularly bogus character. As Allport says, emphasizing his statement with italics: *"Personality means that which is assumed, non-essential, false, as well as that which is vital, inward, and essential."* Philosophers, psychologists, sociologists heatedly debate the issues involved in these contradictions, which of course go far beyond questions of definition; and some of them bear directly on questions of literary interpretation.[21]

We will look at some of these matters later, but for the moment it is important simply to recognize that the polysemous

20. Ian Michael, *English Grammatical Categories and the Tradition to 1800* (Cambridge: Cambridge University Press, 1970), 120.

21. C. G. Jung, "The Persona as a Segment of the Collective Psyche," in *The Relations Between the Ego and the Unconscious,* trans. R. F. C. Hull, in *Collected Works* (New York: Pantheon, 1953), 7:157–58. Kant, *Critique of Practical Reason,* 193. Allport, *Personality,* 29.

character of *persona* and its cognates is responsible for a good deal of the controversy over the term today. To speak of Proust's persona in *Remembrance of Things Past* seems nonsense to critics who maintain that a persona is a mask necessarily representing the opposite of the true self of the writer, or at least a self highly remote from his actual character. For Pope and Swift and others like them, it is the same. About the many possible relationships that may obtain between poet and persona, there is no agreement whatever.[22]

The doctrine of literary sincerity, whose triumphant return has been signaled by Donald Davie and Lionel Trilling, is rooted in tenaciously held beliefs about the nature of the self, the relation of the self to the written word, to the reader, to God. Sincerity, as we shall see in the discusion to follow, can mean many things, but in most definitions it clashes inevitably with ideas of the persona, whether employed functionally by the poet or analytically by the critic. Masks, irony, dissimulation, artifice—all associated with the persona—are suspect when sincerity holds sway.

22. See Ralph W. Rader, "The concept of Genre and Eighteenth-Century Studies," in *New Approaches to Eighteenth-Century Literature: Selected Papers from the English Institute,* ed. Phillip Harth (New York: Columbia University Press, 1974), 93.

Part 2

The Literary Persona

Theory

"It can be argued that all fiction (and poetry and philosophy and painting) ultimately constitutes autobiography, the artist inventing whatever the purported aim of his creation, only a series of metaphors for the self. Conversely, one can maintain that all autobiography is fiction, the imposition of form and the discovery of meaning automatically converting life into its imitation."

Patricia Meyer Spacks, *Imagining a Self: Autobiography and Novel in Eighteenth-Century England* (1976)

3 Sincerity

Embedded deeply in a number of diverse disciplines—ethics, epistemology, psychology and psychoanalysis, aesthetics —the idea of sincerity badly needs full scale, systematic investigation. It will not be an easy task. My own engagement with sincerity is limited. I propose in this chapter to look at some of the ways in which the doctrine of sincerity has impinged and continues to impinge on the use of the first person singular pronoun in literary discourse.

It is embarrassing, but somehow characteristic of the subject, that the most memorable and most influential formulation of what sincerity means to most people should come from a dubious source:

> This above all: to thine own self be true
> And it must follow, as the night the day,
> Thou canst not then be false to any man.

The normative force of Polonius' injunction to Laertes (a force which exists somehow apart from the character of the man who utters it) has been strong in historical periods that were confident in their sense of what the self, to which one should be true, actually is. The ideal of sincerity was imported into literary and critical discourse from the world of ethics. Just as a person's actions should reflect his inner being, so what a writer writes should somehow be consonant with what at bottom he essentially *is*. In the last analysis the writer must be sincere. As we shall see, this ideal, based on views of the self from an earlier day, shows remarkable survival power in the face of a changing poetics as well as Freudian psychoanalysis and various psychological and sociological determinisms powerful in our day. Doubtless its radical ambiguity contributes to its strength.

No one has troubles with the meaning of *insincerity,* which is loaded with negative value—nothing, we believe, is worse than to be insincere—but the word *sincerity* is almost as confusing as *persona*. The literature dealing with the term as it is used in a literary context does not get us far. I. A. Richards has a dozen pages on what he calls "the uncomfortable problem of 'sincerity'" in which he raises some of the necessary questions: How do we determine our own sincerity? "Bogus forms of the virtue waylay us—confident inner assurances and invasive rootless convictions." He deflates one of the most common notions associated with the term, the notion that there is something privileged about simplicity: sincerity is characterized by simple feelings and simple expressions. Thus spontaneous feelings are often held to be more sincere than feelings that have undergone self-criticism; and a dog, says Richards, can be regarded as more sincere than a human being. His remark throws an unkind light on the efforts of surrealist writers to become paradigms of sincerity by giving themselves over completely to the unconscious, circumventing the controls of reason or judgment, as the eighteenth century would say, by means of automatic writing and the hallucinatory agency of drugs. When, however, Richards comes to the positive side of definition, he is forced to turn to a translation of the *Chung Yung* of Confucius, which is not helpful. The closest analog I can find to sincerity as illustrated in Confucius is the innate reason by which Gulliver's Houyhnhnms are blessed. Richards clearly appreciates the inadequacy of our understanding of *sincerity*—still, "Whatever it is, it is the quality we most insistently require in poetry. It is also the quality we most need as critics."[1]

Henry Peyre's *Literature and Sincerity* is a wide-ranging historical survey of Richards's "uncomfortable problem" from classical times to the present in the novels, poems, diaries, journals, letters, autobiographies, and biographies of writers. Not much discrimination among the examples is exercised in Peyre's work. He makes no attempt at formal definition, taking *sincerity* as it comes and where he finds it; and in his own use he slips casually from one sense to another. At the end, after the long, valuable historical survey—he has read everything—Peyre breaks down his last chapter into subheads corresponding to some of the meanings of *sincerity* he has encountered:

> Sincerity through the avoidance of ornaments and of effects, the distrust of style.
> Sincerity as spontaneity, as the deliberate obliteration of what was acquired through education; as liberation from social conformity and moral censorship.
> Sincerity as a refusal of logic and consistency.
> Sincerity conceived as the need to have lived one's work, as identification between the man and the artist.

The list is useful but far from exhaustive, and the discussion touches only lightly on some of the problems underlying the conflicting and ambiguous usage. Finally, although one knows by the end of the book some of the uses of *sincerity* that Peyre deplores, one does not know whether sincerity for him is crucially located in the actions of writers in their daily lives, in their subjective beings, or in the works of art they produce—or possibly in some relationship among these constituents of the sincere life. The book lacks analytic rigor.[2]

Lionel Trilling's remarkable *Sincerity and Authenticity,* to which we will return later, is in a way a celebration of sincerity.

1. I. A. Richards, *Practical Criticism* (New York: Harcourt, Brace, 1929), 280–91.
2. Henri Peyre, *Literature and Sincerity* (New Haven: Yale University Press, 1963). See the review by Vivian Mercier, *Nation,* October 12, 1963, 222–24.

Extremely rigorous in some of its cultural analysis, it is surprisingly relaxed in the way it takes the first of its key terms. Trilling defines *sincerity* as "a congruence between avowal and actual feeling," or again (in a definition applicable to English culture) "communication without deceiving or misleading." He reverts frequently to the formulation by Polonius which assures that one avoids being false to others by being true to one's self. One has no quarrel with any of this, but it is curious that Trilling does not submit *sincerity* to the kind of intense intellectual pressure that he imposes on his second key term, *authenticity*. Instead, he uses *sincerity* in a thin, relatively unproblematic sense. By comparison, *authenticity* is menacingly thick.[3]

Insofar as it affects the use of the first person singular pronoun, the "uncomfortable problem" seems to have arisen in acute form in England in the seventeenth century. We can say with Trilling that *Hamlet* is suffused with the problem of sincerity, and we can ask whether the evident sincerity of Thomas More's Utopian voyager Raphael Hythloday ("For if I wolde speake thynges that be trewe, I muste neades speake suche thinges. But as for to speake false thynges, whether that be a philosophers parte, or no, I can not tel; truely it is not my parte") does not give him a leg up in his debate with the temporizing "More" ("you must with a crafty wile and a subtell trayne studye and endevoure your selfe . . . to handle the matter wittelye and handsomelye for the purpose"); but it is in the seventeenth century that people become manifestly conscious of the problem of how the self should be presented in writing.[4]

Joan Webber in her splendid book *The Eloquent I* is concerned with the use of the self-conscious first person singular pronoun as it appears in a number of nonfictional prose works of seventeenth-century England—among them John Donne's

3. Lionel Trilling, *Sincerity and Authenticity* (Cambridge, Mass.: Harvard University Press, 1971), 2, 58.

4. Sir Thomas More, *The Utopia,* ed. J. H. Lupton (Oxford: Clarendon Press, 1895), 100.

Devotions upon Emergent Occasions, Thomas Browne's *Religio Medici,* Robert Burton's *Anatomy of Melancholy,* John Bunyan's *Grace Abounding to the Chief of Sinners,* John Lilburne's political tracts. Webber selects these particular works because they lack the usual self-protective conventions and thresholds associated with fiction and poetry. In prose nonfiction the interweaving of art and life is tight: the writer is inevitably taken to be who he says he is. It was not a common practice of the seventeenth century for writers to be overtly concerned with the nature of selfhood—these are not Romantic poets struggling to define their own individuality nor twentieth-century novelists searching for a real self among a profusion of masks or in the traces of linguistic codes. Nevertheless, the writers Webber deals with are unremittingly aware that they, as persons, are subjects of their own prose, whether the work is autobiographical or not. Through their "I's" they present themselves.

Webber identifies two distinct categories in the "genre" of self-conscious first person singular prose: the conservative Anglican and the radical Puritan. The "I" of the conservative Anglican is, in her words, "meditative, antihistorical, obscure and ambiguous, symbolic"—a many-sided and confusing configuration because that is the way the Anglican writers conceived of themselves. Donne and Browne are contemplatives, exploring not only their own consciousness but their self-consciousness as well; writing it out (with no sense of the panic to come) like the artist today who says he paints in order to find out what he sees. The Anglican, Webber says, is immensely self-conscious: "Seeing, and seeing that he sees—and is seen; writing, and conscious of the complex relationship betwen the 'I' he thinks of as himself and the 'I' which emerges on paper; conscious too that this relationship—and his attitude toward the literary 'I'—will differ from the reader's, he may produce an 'I' that plays games with the audience, teasing them about his identity in a way that had very seldom been tried in earlier literature."[5]

5. Joan Webber, *The Eloquent 'I': Style and Self in Seventeenth-Century Prose* (Madison: University of Wisconsin Press, 1968), 7, 12–13.

The games are likely to be formidably complex. The *Religio Medici,* for example, gives every appearance of being true intellectual and spiritual autobiography and in many ways it doubtless is; but Browne's first person preface to the reader—the *apologia*—is so thoroughly conventional in theme and tone that it might have been written by any number of authors, whereas the "I" of the treatise that follows is a dazzlingly complex creation, certainly unique, and related in the most ambiguous ways to the historical Thomas Browne. In a famous passage Browne writes that he has never married, that he would be happy if we human beings could procreate like trees instead of by the "triviall and vulgar way of coition . . . the foolishest act a wise man commits in all his life." At the time he composed the passage, Browne was indeed not married; but he was married well before the first authorized publication of the *Religio,* for which he had carefully revised his text, and he allowed the statement to stand. It continued to stand through eight editions in his lifetime and the birth of twelve children. Clearly, despite the use of the first person singular and the undeniable self-reference of much of the work, the *Religio* cannot be thought of as literal autobiography. The "I" of the work is impossible to pin down as identical with the author; it is a construct, a *trompe l'œil,* Webber calls it. I suppose one could say that Browne is not "sincere" in making the claims about marriage and the travails of coition; but whether such a judgment would be useful or not is a question.[6]

Robert Burton, writing of melancholy to avoid melancholy, masks himself under the visard, as he says, of Democritus Junior; that is, he personates the melancholy philosopher of Greece who laughed at all he saw, and takes on Democritus' name to protect his own true identity: "I would not willingly be known." At the end of the first edition, however, in a highly conventional *apologia,* he changes his mind and signs himself "Robert Burton, From my study in Christ Church, Oxon., Dec. 5, 1620." In between, Burton has taken nearly every position one can think of (except direct confession) with respect to

6. Webber, *Eloquent 'I,'* 153–57.

his "I." Self-concealment, he says, is hopeless: "our style be-wrays us, and as hunters find their game by the trace, so is a man's *genius* descried by his works; we judge much better of a man's character by his words than by his features. . . . I have laid myself open (I know it) in this treatise, turned mine inside out-ward." If anyone wants to know, he continues, if I, who censure others, think myself faultless, I have more faults than any reader: "I am as foolish, as mad as any one." To those who criticize me, I will answer, with Erasmus, "'Tis not I, but Democritus who said it: you must consider what it is to speak in another's per-son." Why may I not speak my mind freely? If you deny me this liberty,

> upon these presumptions I will take it: I say again I will take it. . . . I owe thee nothing (Reader) . . . I am independent, I fear not.
>   No, I recant, I will not, I care, I fear. . . . I have spoken foolishly, rashly. . . . absurdly, I have anatomized mine own folly. And now . . . I am awakened as it were out of a dream. . . . Absolve me, pardon (O kind readers).[7]

And so—a thousand changes rung on the first person pro-noun, the intermittent references to the actual Robert Burton providing a kind of historical baseline, but for the rest a con-trolled chaos, stage-managed up to the absurdly ambiguous biographical-literary end by Democritus Junior. Robert Bur-ton's epitaph, composed by himself and inscribed on his bust in Christ Church Chapel, Oxford, reads as follows: "Paucis notus, paucioribus ignotus, hic jacet Democritus Junior, cui vitam dedit et mortem Melancholia" (Known to few [as Burton], unknown to fewer [as Democritus], here lies Democritus Junior, to whom Melancholy gave life and death). As Webber says, if Democritus is wholly a created character, a persona in that sense, then the epitaph is nonsense: a fictional character does not die just because the author dies. "But if Burton *is* Democritus Junior, then he is

    7. Robert Burton, *The Anatomy of Melancholy,* ed. Floyd Dell and Paul Jordan-Smith, 2 vols. (New York: George H. Doran, 1927), 1:11, 21, 101, 102, 103–4.

both a 'real' person and a persona, hence both mortal and im-
mortal." As for sincerity, once again it is not an issue as Burton
plays his intricate games with the reader.[8]

One finds no such games among the Puritans. In Webber's
analysis the radical Puritan "I" is at the opposite extreme; it is
"active, timebound, as simple and visible as possible, desirous of
being taken literally and seriously as a man living in a hostile
world." The presentation is less sophisticated than the Anglican, less mannered—plain, even crude, as direct as these things
can be. John Lilburne, the Leveller, refuses to make any distinction between the "I" of his prose and "John Lilburne as ever I
was in my life." Webber shows conclusively that Lilburne intends "to be one person, to play one role, in print or out, in
public, in private, in life and art, to make thoughts, feelings,
writings and actions match." In short, he intends to be sincere.
Whereas the "I" of the Anglicans is consciously a rhetorical
construct, a persona as we would say—think of Donne's witty,
mannered presentation of himself in the *Devotions,* written when
he thought he was dying—the Puritan wants to reduce to nothing the boundary between life and the expression of life on the
printed page, to make the public and the private man coincide.
No matter how hard he tries to present himself whole, however,
to show himself, without bias, in his written work, the Puritan
too necessarily creates a persona; for the details he presents have
been selected, consciously or unconsciously, from an infinite
number of possible details, and the "I" of the text can never be
identical with its creator. Nevertheless, in the creation of that
persona the Puritan gives us a paradigm of sincerity.[9]

Curiously, both Donne and Bunyan, splendid examples of
their kinds, have been accused of insincerity. Scholars have
shown that Bunyan's report of his conversion experience falls
into a traditional Puritan pattern. Donne has been accused, in his

8. Douglas Bush, *English Literature in the Earlier Seventeenth Century* (Oxford:
Clarendon Press, 1945), 280. Webber, *Eloquent 'I,'* 80.
9. Webber, *Eloquent 'I,'* 8, 57–58.

own day as well as later, of wielding rhetoric too deftly, of being too much taken with the show of words. "If Bunyan was too imitative, Donne was too mannered," writes Webber; "in both cases, such criticism really implies, there is a lack of spontaneity, a striving for effect at the expense of truth to experience"—in our terms, a lack of sincerity.[10]

The effort to match inner and outer man, so strong in the work of Lilburne, Bunyan, and others of their persuasion, leaves an ineradicable mark on succeeding literature. It was indeed something new—or relatively new—under the sun. Classical literary doctrine assumed no necessary connection between the most intense personal poems and the lives or personalities of their authors. The Roman elegists, for example—Catullus, Propertius—write of their mistresses with memorable passion; to our ears the poems seem openly confessional, "sincere," as the poets declare their love; yet modern scholars have shown the folly of reading even the marvelous poems to Lesbia as autobiographical documents. Despite its personal form, erotic poetry cannot be taken to reflect the true feelings or conduct of the writer. There are conventions for love poetry as for other forms of artistic expression, and the poets themselves insist on the distinction between art and life. "The true poet should be chaste himself; his verses need not be," writes Catullus; and both Ovid and Martial claim they lead pure lives despite the erotic experiences described in their verse. Such claims are probably to be taken no more literally than the oaths of undying devotion to the Cynthia of the minute, but this is not to say that the poets were insincere. For them sincerity is a function of style, involving a relation between the artist and the public; it has to do with the presentation of a self appropriate to the kind of verse being written, to the genre, not with the personality of the poet.[11]

10. Webber, *Eloquent 'I,'* 271, n. 5.
11. Archibald W. Allen, "Sunt Qui Propertium Malint," in J. P. Sullivan, ed., *Critical Essays on Roman Literature: Elegy and Lyric* (London: Routledge and Kegan Paul, 1962), 107–48. Rosalie Colie points out that the apparently blatant sincerity of Sidney's "'Foole,' said my Muse to me, 'looke in thy heart and

Similarly, there is no evidence that the Roman audience expected a poet like Juvenal to write satires in which the feelings expressed had necessarily to grow out of his own actual experience. Juvenal may in fact have suffered grievously from the snobberies and betrayals of high-born ladies, as in Gilbert Highet's interpretation; he may have been victimized outrageously by the corruption endemic in Nero's Rome; but the only evidence we have supporting such conclusions are the artistically controlled expressions of *saeva indignatio* we find in his poems. Apart from that we know nothing of his personality. The accusations about his insincerity as a poet, and the conclusion that he was homosexual, are based on misunderstanding of his rhetorical procedures.[12]

I have sometimes thought that the most sincere poems of all are those of blessing and cursing promulgated in a culture that believes without qualification in their magical or religious efficacy. Ethnographers are the curators of the true poetry of sincerity. Perhaps Archilochus in the seventh century B. C. really believed that his great curse uttered against "him who was once my friend" would bring the man to his doom. The poem sounds as though all the sincerity of hate and all the confidence in hate's malign efficacy are behind it, but of course one cannot know. No more can one know about the character of the passion behind some of Archilochus' lyric fragments. K. J. Dover warns against our assumption "that whenever a fragment of an early Greek poet contains a first person singular it comes from a genuinely autobiographical poem." Archilochus lived in a time of transition from preliteracy to literacy. Emotions expressed in the preliterate songs forming the tradition to which he was

---

write'!" derives in fact from Ronsard, thus emphasizing the "conventional nature of poetic honesty." *Paradoxia Epidemica: the Renaissance Tradition of Paradox* (Princeton: Princeton University Press, 1966), 91; cf. 360.

12. Gilbert Highet, *Juvenal The Satirist* (Oxford: Clarendon Press, 1954), 103, 269, n. 17; cf. William S. Anderson's criticism of Highet's approach and his analysis of Juvenal's persona in *Anger in Juvenal and Seneca,* University of California Publications in Classical Philology 19 (Berkeley, University of California), 143ff.

heir were not necessarily the emotions of the composer. As for another kind of intensely "personal" poetry, that of Greek homosexuality, Dover writes this: "By 'the poet' I mean the *persona* adopted for the purpose of composition; we do not know which poems, if any, express the feelings of their composers for actual boys at any given time." In ancient literatures it is the personality expressed in the poem, not the personality of the historical poet, that signifies.[13]

Nothing could be further, of course, from the attitude toward the self, and the self's relation to others, fostered by the Puritans. It is impossible to know how directly influential their attitudes were, although unquestionably those attitudes took root in the English consciousness and have flourished, sometimes in odd places, since. Certainly no Puritan, John Dryden is capable of evaluating Roman satirists on the basis of norms similar to theirs: "There is a Spirit of sincerity in all [Persius] says: You may easily discern that he is in earnest, and is perswaded of that Truth which he inculcates. In this I am of opinion, that he excels *Horace,* who is commonly in jeast." Thus in Dryden's view Persius not only conveys a feeling of sincerity in his poems, he actually believes in the doctrines about which he writes; his superiority over Horace in this respect is a moral superiority. Toward the end of his long assessment of the Roman satirists, Dryden finally concludes that Horace, despite his irreverent jesting, was a greater poet than Persius, thus setting himself apart from the many critics in succeeding years who awarded literary preeminence on the basis of imputed moral characteristics.[14]

Once enunciated, sincerity was a virtue hard to deny.

13. For the curse and discussion see Robert C. Elliott, *The Power of Satire,* 285–92. K. J. Dover, "The Poetry of Archilochos," in *Archiloque: sept exposés et discussions,* Entretiens sur l'antiquité classique, 10 (Geneva: Fondation Hardt, 1964), 183–222. Dover, *Greek Homosexuality* (Cambridge, Mass.: Harvard University Press, 1978), 58, n. 32.

14. John Dryden, "Discourse Concerning the Original and Progress of Satire," ed. William Frost, in *Works* (Berkeley: University of California Press, 1974), 4:57.

Eighteenth-century philosophers of primitivism held that one of the reasons for the relative superiority of barbarism over civilization is that, as Hugh Blair said, in the infancy of society people "display themselves to one another without disguise: and converse and act in the uncovered simplicity of nature." From this point of view there are no personae in the infancy of society, and in one way the eighteenth-century literature of sensibility is an effort to return to that happy state. The more skeptical representatives of the period, on the other hand, were likely to have little use for such simplicities, evincing instead a healthy respect for role playing and even for a judicious touch of hypocrisy. Swift's authoritarian "Project for the Advancement of Religion and the Reformation of Manners" advocates making the profession of religion and morality a necessary step in preferment. Men will personate any virtue in order to get ahead, he maintains; the attendant hypocrisy may even be beneficial: "I believe, it is often with Religion as it is with Love; which, by much Dissembling, at last grows real."[15]

David Hume believed that people could not survive in society without exercising a certain amount of hypocrisy—the other side of Freud's later belief that hypocrisy (again, a certain amount only) is indispensable for civilization. And Benjamin Franklin, America's great Enlightenment figure, consciously, openly, unabashedly played roles, "with some violence," he said, "to natural Inclination." Franklin added Humility to his list of virtues; he writes in his *Autobiography*: "I cannot boast of much success in acquiring the *reality* of this virtue, but I had

15. Hugh Blair, *Critical Dissertation on . . . Ossian* (London: for T. Becket and P. A. De Hondt, 1763), 2–3. Jonathan Swift, "A Project for the Advancement of Religion and the Reformation of Manners" (1709), in *Prose Works,* ed. Herbert Davis (Oxford: Basil Blackwell, 1957), 2:57. Another moralist, André Gide, expresses similar sentiments: "Often you become what you want to be, and you eventually really experience the feeling that you began by pretending to experience. . . . And how many people, just because they thought themselves devout or in love, soon became sincerely devout or in love!" *Journals,* trans. Justin O'Brien (New York: Knopf, 1948), 2:413. Gide works this idea into *The Counterfeiters* in the characterization of Pastor Vedel. Max Beerbohm's story "The Happy Hypocrite" plays with wit and delicacy on these themes.

a good deal with regard to the *appearance* of it." Such candor inevitably invited accusations of hypocrisy from later Romantic writers like Melville and D. H. Lawrence.[16]

The Romantics and the Victorians are, of course, the true heirs of the Puritans in these matters; but conventional categories often do not hold up, and one of the major ideological successors to John Lilburne is Samuel Johnson. For Johnson, as for the Puritans, the inner man and the outer must coincide: the poet must feel the emotions he expresses. Love poems contrived from the stock of traditional imagery are false as the characters of those who contrive them. "He that courts his mistress with Roman imagery deserves to lose her; for she may with good reason suspect his sincerity." Jean Hagstrum speaks of Johnson's relentless and literal-minded application of the doctrine of sincerity to literary criticism. It is the source of his notorious denunciation of Milton's *Lycidas,* which "is not to be considered as the effusion of real passion; for passion runs not after remote allusions and obscure opinions. Passion plucks no berries from the myrtle and ivy . . . nor tells of rough *satyrs* and *fauns with cloven heel.* Where there is leisure for fiction there is little grief. In this poem there is no nature, for there is no truth." An embarrassing example in so great a critic of sincerity's reductive influence.[17]

It is the more surprising therefore to find Johnson in the final isue of the *Rambler* speaking in favor of literary disguise. He points to the privilege of the nameless writer and cites authority: "'a mask,' says Castiglione, 'confers a right of acting and speaking with less restraint, even when the wearer happens to be known.'" Johnson's anonymity in the *Rambler* releases him from the strict accountability of sincerity.

Despite these anticipations, until the nineteenth century the word *sincerity* in England had to do primarily with religion, with

16. See Judith Shklar's splendid essay, "Let Us Not Be Hypocritical," *Daedalus,* Summer 1979, 1–25.

17. Jean Hagstrum, *Samuel Johnson's Literary Criticism* (Minneapolis: University of Minnesota Press, 1952), 44–47.

purity of belief and freedom from theological duplicity or corruption. Wordsworth (who shared Dr. Johnson's distaste for Petrarchian love poetry) is generally thought to have made the significant bridge from religion to poetry: in his essays "Upon Epitaphs" he insisted that the writer of commemorative poetry must have a devout heart; we judge the poem depending upon "our opinion or feeling of the Author's state of mind." Patricia Ball points out, however, that Wordsworth did not equate the sentiments of the devout heart with poetic value: that was to come later in the century; the sentiments, presumably, were a necessary but not a sufficient condition of good poetry, although how Wordsworth or any reader was to gain access to them except through the poetry itself is left at this point unanswered. Ball maintains that although the Romantic poets speak of sincerity, it is usually not in connection with poetry. True, they believe that poetry emerges from an intense inner experience impossible to simulate; that in order to express deep emotion a poet must have felt deeply, so that in this psychological sense there is a correspondence between what is said on the page and what has been felt by the poet; but ordinarily they do not use the word *sincerity* to characterize this process. *Sincerity* becomes a major critical term in the 1830s and later when Victorian critics attach edifyingly moral overtones to the Romantic notions of the creative process. The result, says Ball: "a confused emotional-moral test for literature imposed without qualification, and the adulterating of an idea concerned at its inception with the study of the creative mind and the genesis of poems."[18]

For Carlyle, Dante is a great poet because he is sincere. A Romantic poet might have said that the *Divine Comedy* "came deep out of the author's heart of hearts; and it goes deep into ours," but then Carlyle goes on to make a mystique of sincerity:

18. Johnson's comment is cited in Meyer H. Abrams, "Poetic Truth and Sincerity," *The Mirror and the Lamp* (New York: Oxford University Press, 1953), 312–20. Patricia M. Ball, "Sincerity: The Rise and Fall of a Literary Term," *Modern Language Review* 59 (1964): 1–2; cf. David Perkins, "The Challenge of Sincerity," in *Wordsworth and the Poetry of Sincerity* (Cambridge, Mass.: Harvard University Press, 1964), 1–32.

"the eye flashes direct into the heart of things and *sees* the truth of them . . . Great Nature's own gift . . . what I call sincerity of vision." There is "something of divine" in sincerity; it is "the measure of worth." As Ball says, this is reduction by apotheosis. From Carlyle it is but a short step to the belief, familiar, I daresay, to all readers of this book, that sincerity is a sufficient condition for the writing of poetry.[19]

In France the doctrine of literary sincerity had a moralistic bias similar to that in England but not as overwhelming, despite the egregious example of Molière's Alceste. Rousseau (whom W. K. Wimsatt calls an avatar of Alceste) is of course the central figure in the French tradition. Kant honored Rousseau for distinguishing more clearly than other philosophers had done between the masks man has created for himself throughout history and what is essential in man, his ethical nature. A major task of Rousseau's life was to eliminate his own mask, to present himself to the world, as he boasts at the beginning of the *Confessions,* "in all the integrity of nature." His example was immensely influential in establishing the cult sincerity, in France and in every area of the world touched by French thought. As Henri Peyre convincingly shows, the dogma of sincerity—ambiguous, contradictory, unclear as it is—affects the work of nearly every major writer and critic of the last two centuries. Taine prefers the work of Musset to that of Tennyson because Musset "was more than a poet, he was a man"—an agonizingly sincere man. Stendhal's lifelong search for subjective sincerity, recorded amply in his journals and letters and autobiographical works, leads to the most acute doubts: does he really know himself? At the heart of Stendhal's autobiographical fiction *La Vie de Henri Burlard* is a sincerity that is at once the source of the work's great appeal and at the same time always in question.

Ambiguously self-referential works of this kind raise the most difficult questions: they do this in any case, but the difficulties are compounded when sincerity is an issue. If the sincere writer

19. Ball, "Sincerity," 3.

must tell the truth about himself, what kind of truth is demanded in fictional autobiographies—historical truth, psychological truth, fictional truth? What does fictional truth mean in this context? If the author writes in the first person even under a transparent pseudonym, must he have felt the emotions and lived the experiences he describes? Must the poet's "I" be truly I—if he is Baudelaire, must he be a satanist? If Henry Miller, a sexual athlete? And, perhaps most perplexing of all, can a poet contrive diligently to be sincere? can he labor to give the impression of sincerity and still be sincere? Paul Valéry maintained that the poet need not have experienced the emotion described in the poem in any degree, so long as he created it in his readers—an effort requiring the most exquisite artifice.

To serious people the demands of sincerity are unremitting and cruel, the source of great personal suffering: the "malady of sincerity," a young friend of André Gide's called it. Gide, Paul Claudel, and Paul Valéry, close friends when young, sharing similar literary tastes, came to have sharply different attitudes toward sincerity. (Henri Peyre says that the three friends "parted ways" and became mutually distrustful over the issue, but that seems overstated, at least as far as Gide and Valéry are concerned.) The following entry in Gide's *Journal* indicates how central the doctrine of sincerity was to his intellectual and spiritual life, and how tormenting. He returns to the theme many times:

> When one has begun to write, the hardest thing is to be sincere. Essential to mull over that idea and to define artistic sincerity. Meanwhile, I hit upon this: the word must never precede the idea. Or else: the word must always be necessitated by the idea. It must be irresistible and inevitable; and the same is true of the sentence, of the whole work of art. And for the artist's whole life.... The fear of not being sincere has been tormenting me for several months and preventing me from writing. Oh, to be utterly and perfectly sincere.

Claudel, on the other hand, felt that constant introspection, searching for sincerity, was unhealthy. "We falsify ourselves through watching ourselves," he wrote in 1925, "and fabricate a sort of artificial person which is substituted for the other." As for Valéry, sincerity with oneself is an illusion, a comic illusion when it is paraded for effect, as with Stendhal: "so much sincerity coupled with a little too much life." By trying to be sincere, to be genuine, Stendhal falsifies himself. "The genuineness he strives to promote changes under his pen into a tone designed to appear genuine"—the inevitable fate of such efforts. Individuals can be sincere with each other, but as soon as one thinks of being sincere to oneself, the will to that end necessarily brings with it a principle of falsification. Thus Stendhal's vaunted sincerity was part of the "comedy of sincerity" he played for himself.[20]

In England, attacks on the simplistic notion of sincerity associated with the Victorians multiplied as the nineteenth century gave way to the twentieth. "All bad poetry springs from genuine feeling," said Oscar Wilde, and in the "Decay of Lying" he fervently praises (through his mouthpiece Vivian) "the glory of mendacity," the superiority of the mask to the reality behind the mask. Doubtless, as Robert Langbaum suggests, the twentieth century's preoccupation with masks and roles may be explained in part as a reaction to the exaltation of sincerity in the preceding age.[21]

In any case, the great wave of The Modern which swept over England and the United States after World War I altered to a very considerable degree what the word *sincerity* meant to sophisticated literary people. Debased by loose and extravagant usage, it still had a strong (if unexamined) ethical content; but its application to artistic work was understood to be a complicated

20. Peyre, *Literature and Sincerity*, 265. Gide, *Journals*, trans. O'Brien, 1:16–17. Paul Valéry, "Stendhal," in *Masters and Friends*, trans. Martin Turnell, vol. 9 of *The Collected Works*, sponsored by the Bollingen Foundation (Princeton: Princeton University Press, 1968), 195ff. In another context Valéry says what we will see others saying about the same phenomenon: "Intentional sincerity leads to the kind of reflection which leads to doubt, which leads to nothingness." Cited by Robert Mallet in his Introduction to *Self-Portraits: the Gide/Valéry Letters*, trans. June Guicharnaud (Chicago: University of Chicago Press, 1966), 20.

21. Robert Langbaum, *The Mysteries of Identity* (New York: Oxford University Press, 1977), 13.

and risky matter, vulnerable in a high degree to irony. With some notable exceptions, the term *sincerity* was not much used by leading writers and critics. An F. R. Leavis might in all seriousness distinguish between the sincere and insincere aspects of T. S. Eliot's work; but this, as Lionel Trilling says, is merely evidence of the engagingly archaic quality of Leavis' seriousness. However, the word survived as a critical term at another level. In the 1920s and early 1930s, when he was writing *Practical Criticism,* I. A. Richards found that *sincerity* was a key word in the papers of students who were asked to write critically of unfamiliar poetry. For them it was a strong, value-laden term, but hopelessly vague; and so it remains for our students today. Patricia Ball has noticed that the word still appears frequently in the pages of *TLS* devoted to one-paragraph assessments of novels. Presumably the intention of the critics is to say something benevolent, to recognize a certain degree of skill in the work under consideration, but to place it in an unmistakably minor category. Here, in this "rather forlorn area between imaginative art and popular trade work" *sincerity* survived in our time as a critical term until its recent resuscitation.[22]

The occasion of the revival was the startling shift in poetic and critical sensibility associated with the poetic revolution undertaken in the 1950s and 1960s by poets like Robert Lowell, W. D. Snodgrass, Allen Ginsberg, Sylvia Plath, Randell Jarrell, John Berryman—poets who deliberately and sometimes after great struggle rejected the dominant modernist aesthetic, with its prescriptive impersonality, in favor of a breakthrough back into life, as they said, into the immediate, personal, usually painful life experience of the poet. Confessional poetry—so this work came to be called—raised once more questions that New Critical stringency had seemed to have safely laid to rest.

Donald Davie is a strong proponent of reintroducing *sincerity* as a critical norm. In an influential article, "On Sincerity: from Wordsworth to Ginsberg," published in *Encounter* in 1968,

---

22. Ball, "Sincerity," 9.

Davie says that despite all the difficulties and confusions attendant on so ambiguous a term, the new poetry of confession absolutely requires the reinstitution of sincerity as a norm for poetry. He instances Robert Lowell, a poet trained in the heart of the New Criticism by Allen Tate, one whose early work conformed fully to modernist principles in its impersonality, its use of an "I" in the poems remote from the actual poet—a poet who in *Life Studies* (1959) suddenly threw off the old formalisms, including the persona, and wrote in the new confessional mode. Lowell's "I" in *Life Studies,* says Davie, asks to be taken, unequivocally, as the historical Robert Lowell, as the poet himself. Once again in this kind of poetry, Davie concedes, the public life and the private life of a poet are messily compounded; but "the question of sincerity can never again be out of order." It is not easy to say exactly what Davie intends by the word *sincerity.* At the end of the essay it has come to mean control of tone and other technical elements of a poem, but his leading sense involves a direct correspondence between the "I" of the poem and the person of the author. The idea of the persona taken from Pound, the closely related idea of the mask taken from Yeats, Eliot's ideas that the structure of a poem is inherently a dramatic structure and that the poem is an escape from personality—these ideas, says Davie, must be abandoned. He welcomes the new dispensation.

So does Lionel Trilling in his eloquent and moving book *Sincerity and Authenticity.* With some asperity in his tone Trilling deconstructs—a word he would not have used—the modern mystique of impersonality. He is particularly severe on the critical insistence "that the poet is not a person at all, only a *persona,* and that to impute to him a personal existence is a breach of literary decorum."

This chaste view of literature doubtless had its corrective uses. But the day seems to have passed when the simple truth that criticism is not gossip requires to be enforced by precepts which forbid us to mark the resemblances between Stephen Dedalus and James Joyce or between Michel or Jérome and

André Gide. We are no longer required to regard as wholly fortuitous the fact that the hero of Proust's novel is named Marcel. Within the last two decades English and American poets have progammatically scuttled the sacred doctrine of the *persona,* the belief that the poet does not, must not, present himself to us and figure in our consciousness as a person, as a man speaking to men, but must have an exclusively aesthetic existence.

Like Davie, Trilling believes that the scuttling of the persona has been accomplished by those poets for whom the unmediated exhibition of the self is central, the poets who write confessional poetry.[23]

In my view these obsequies over the doctrine of the persona are premature and in large part misconceived; indeed, I would think the example of confessional poetry points up the necessity for such a doctrine in a peculiarly poignant way. I propose to look at some issues raised by Robert Lowell's *Life Studies* which are directly to the point.

Lowell is completely candid about his break with the impersonal, hieratic style in which he established his reputation. There came a time in his life when what he called the Alexandrian tradition in which he had written stifled him; he had to find a way to break through the shell of his old manner, back, as he said, into life. His way was to adopt a new, highly personal subject matter and to work out, through intense struggle, a style suited to it—he called it a revolutionary style. When *Life Studies* appeared in 1959 it shocked some reviewers and many readers. It was blatantly autobiographical, dealing with the kind of personal, intimate, sometimes shameful matters that floated as gossip around New York cocktail parties—emphatically not the proper stuff of poetry. M. L. Rosenthal in what has become a famous review wrote that whereas Eliot and Pound masked their psyches from greedy eyes, "Lowell removes the mask. His speaker is unequivocally himself, and it is hard not to think of *Life Studies* as a series of personal confidences, rather shameful,

23. Trilling, *Sincerity and Authenticity,* 8.

that one is honor-bound not to reveal." Many readers find that a substantial part of the fascination, the strength, the poignancy of these poems resides in their claim to truth—truth about their author, his miserable childhood, his conflictual marriage, his terrible bouts with madness. The experience of the poems is Robert Lowell's experience. The "I" is unequivocally—scores of critics have made the equation—his.[24]

And of course in some sense all this is true; but in another sense it is not true at all, which makes for a nasty dilemma. For example, in a recent book on Lowell, Steven Axelrod writes of "My Last Afternoon with Uncle Devereux Winslow," one of the poems of *Life Studies,* that it "cleaves . . . to the literal, particular, time-bound world of fact." Unlike most autobiographical writing, Axelrod says, it is anything but euphemistic or evasive; it resists deception and self-deception—in short, it presents autobiographical truth unvarnished. Yet in an adjacent paragraph Axelrod concedes that the factual accuracy of the autobiographical poems is by no means clear. He cites key phrases from Lowell's own comments made to an interviewer from the *Paris Review:* the poems from *Life Studies,* Lowell told the interviewer, are

> not always factually true. There's a good deal of tinkering with fact. You leave out a lot, and emphasize this and not that. Your actual experience is a complete flux. I've invented facts and changed things. . . . Yet . . . if a poem is autobiographical . . . you want the reader to say, this is true. . . . And so there was always that standard of truth which you wouldn't ordinarily have in poetry—the reader was to believe he was getting the *real* Robert Lowell.

Axelrod juxtaposes the conflicting claims with no attempt to reconcile them: he prints Lowell's statements about factuality, but then ignores their import.[25]

24. M. L. Rosenthal, "Poetry as Confession," *Nation* 189 (September 19, 1959): 154.
25. Steven Gould Axelrod, *Robert Lowell: Life and Art* (Princeton: Princeton University Press, 1978), 111–13. Frederick Seidel's Interview with Robert Low-

The dilemma can be pointed up and made more concrete by a look at "Skunk Hour," the last poem in *Life Studies,* one of the most celebrated of all Robert Lowell's poems. The first four stanzas of "Skunk Hour" describe, indirectly, the decayed condition of "our village," a seacoast town in Maine. Quick sketches of local personalities—the "hermit heiress," the "summer millionaire," the "fairy decorator"—are handled almost laconically. Lowell said of these early stanzas, "Sterility howls through the scenery, but I try to give a tone of tolerance, humor, and randomness to the sad prospect." The tone tightens fiercely in stanzas five and six as the speaker focuses on himself, his torment:

> One dark night,
> my Tudor Ford climbed the hill's skull;
> I watched for love-cars. Lights turned down,
> they lay together, hull to hull,
> where the graveyard shelves on the town. . . .
> My mind's not right.
>
> A car radio bleats,
> "Love, O careless Love. . . ." I hear
> my ill-spirit sob in each blood cell,
> as if my hand were at its throat. . . .
> I myself am hell; . . .

Confessional poetry can hardly go further. Here are no personae, writes Richard Wilbur: the poet speaks of and for himself; he remembers the "prurient yearning" with which one dark night he spied on love cars; he is moved by a "paroxysm of balked desire." "I" and author are unequivocally the same. Here, we must conclude, is the true poetry of sincerity.[26]

Lowell's own comments on "Skunk Hour" disrupt the simple straightforwardness of this formulation. "I found the bleak personal violence [of the last stanzas of the poem] repellent," he writes. "All was too close, though watching the lovers was not

ell, *Paris Review* 25 (1961–62): 71; reprinted in *Writers at Work: The Paris Review Interviews,* 2d series, ed. George Plimpton (New York: Viking, 1963).

26. Richard Wilbur, "On Robert Lowell's 'Skunk Hour,'" in *The Contemporary Poet as Artist and Critic,* ed. Anthony Ostroff (Boston: Little, Brown, 1964), 86.

mine, but from an anecdote on Walt Whitman in his old age. I began to feel that real poetry came, not from fierce confessions, but from something almost meaningless but imagined." A statement like that tests the new poetics of sincerity—the unequivocal identification of "I" and author—to the limit. Can a criterion of sincerity appropriately be invoked when at the level of the "literal, particular, time-bound world of fact" the poem makes false assertions about its author? David Kalstone writes that in stanza five the troubled "I" of the poet enters undisguised; but as Denis Donoghue points out, the poet's "I" on the contrary is very heavily disguised indeed: what the "I" of the poem confesses to doing, Robert Lowell denies having done.[27]

If we take "Skunk Hour" as an example of confessional poetry, as in some sense it unquestionably is, it is possible to suppose that Lowell takes upon himself, in the poem, a perverse action attributed in an anecdote to Walt Whitman (an action of which Lowell himself was, in a literal sense, innocent) in order to evoke some truth about himself. Such an act might be undertaken in the name of the higher sincerity. At a grubbier level, however, we have sheer unescapable embarrassment. Do we really want to ask if Lowell was *sincere* when he wrote "I watched for love-cars"? Lionel Trilling says that telling the truth about oneself to oneself and to others, including the shameful truth, constitutes sincerity in French literature. The English require of the sincere person, he says, only communication without deceiving or misleading. By either standard Robert Lowell fails. But if Lowell is not sincere, do we want to go on and say that he lied in confessing to something he did not do? Or that he lied when, in his comment on "Skunk Hour," he denied that the act of voyeurism was his? Are these the appropriate questions to be putting to a major poem and a major poet? Assuredly they are not.[28]

Questions of this order arise inevitably when "I" and author

27. Robert Lowell, "On 'Skunk Hour,'" in Ostroff, 109–10. David Kalstone, *Five Temperaments* (New York: Oxford University Press, 1977), 50. See Denis Donoghue's review in *Times Literary Supplement,* July 21, 1978, 810.

28. Trilling, *Sincerity and Authenticity,* 58.

are unequivocally identified and when, as a result of that identification, sincerity becomes an issue. In writing his poem Robert Lowell (and many poets like him) was playing against a standard of truth to which the terms *sincerity* and *confession* apply only in the most carefully qualified senses. His truth admitted of inventing facts and changing things about so that the reader would think he was getting another kind of truth—the *real* Robert Lowell. But the reader's Lowell is necessarily, in part, a fiction.[29]

John Berryman's reading of "Skunk Hour" resolves the dilemma. The occasion of "Skunk Hour," Berryman writes, is the approach of a crisis of mental disorder for the speaker of the poem. It is certain, he says, that we are dealing here with Robert Lowell's personal experience, not with invention and symbol. On the other hand, the "I" of the poem can never be identical with the actual author who has a local habitation and a Social Security number and duties and debts and a thousand involvements remote from any particular poem. The poet who writes about himself must select from the vast flux of his experience. When Shakespeare writes, "Two loves I have," he does not mean, says Berryman, that he has only two, for he must also have loved others: his children, parents, wife, mistress, friends—who knows? "The necessity for the artist of selection opens inevitably an abyss between his person and his persona." No matter how closely the poetry is about the poet, the gap is there. "The persona looks across at the person and then sets about its own work." Thus in Berryman's view the "I" of Lowell's poems both is and is not identical with the author. An empirical but also a poetic "I," it need not be held to factual accuracy or to the literal correspondences of sincerity. The significance of this double aspect of the "I" is movingly illuminated by Berryman in an intensely personal comment: "This

29. Cf. James Merrill: "Confessional poetry . . . is a literary convention like any other, the problem being to make it *sound* as if it were true," to produce the "illusion of a True Confession." Donald Sheehan, "An Interview with James Merrill," *Contemporary Literature* 9 (Winter 1968): 1–2.

mysterious 'I' that poets deploy can certainly never be defined,
but . . . I would call it virtually certain that Lowell had in mind
and at heart during this poem not only his own difficulties
whatever they may be or have been but the personal disorders
to which other poets of his age and place have been furiously
subject.[30]

Robert Lowell's use of the first person singular pronoun is
linked in its double agency—the "I" of agonized personal experience but also the "I" representative of an age, a terrible
age—with the uses of Dante and Juan Ruiz and Chaucer and
Pope and with writers as dissimilar, and yet as much alike in
their "creative autobiographies," as Wordsworth and Proust. If
one wants to use the term, one can say that Lowell writes confessional poetry; but we must remember that confessional poetry
is poetry, not life. Words like *confession* and *sincerity* used in this
context must have flags on them—they must be given highly
specific, carefully controlled meanings or we inevitably find ourselves floundering in categorical confusions of the kind that
claim confessional poetry has scuttled the persona. Lowell's case
demonstrates that the contrary is true: if anything, confessional
poetry establishes the persona's indispensability.

As for sincerity, it is in many ways a dubious ideal, not only
in literature. For one thing, it leaves out so much. I. A. Richards is one of the few analysts who have tried to accommodate
irony, "where the feeling really present [in the writer] is often
the exact contrary to that overtly expressed," under a standard of
sincerity. Most upholders of that standard remind me of Sophia
Antonovna, the revolutionary in Conrad's *Under Western Eyes:*
"'Remember, Razumov,'" she cries passionately, "'that women, children, and revolutionists hate irony, which is the ne-
gation of all saving instincts, of all faith, of all devotion, of all
action,'" A totally sincere man like Werther cannot begin to

---

30. John Berryman, "Despondency and Madness: on Robert Lowell's 'Skunk
Hour,'" in Ostroff, 99–106.

cope with irony. In the revolution which reestablishes sincerity as a necessary condition of good poetry, Donald Davie warns us that we must learn to set less store by irony and paradox than we have in the past. Herbert Read gives definitive expression to the point of view hostile to irony in an essay on Jonathan Swift: "Irony is a fashionable mode, and has to-day an esteem such as it also had in the eighteenth century. It is in this sense the hallmark of an insincere age; and though Swift is the last man to be accused of a lack of sincerity, yet this provocative display of indirectness is the counterpart of a certain defect of character." A relatively unexamined principle itself, sincerity prescribes some notable exclusions.[31]

Philosophical analysis exposes some of the weaknesses of sincerity as an ethical ideal. Sartre instances it as a phenomenon of bad faith. A rough summary of Stuart Hampshire's examination of sincerity, which points up some of the epistemological problems, would go something like this: Chamfort's injunction, "One must not watch oneself living," proclaims an ideal of sincerity. Naturalness and spontaneity are, in this view, incompatible with self-watching, which tends to make one morbidly self-conscious. If instead of feeling something spontaneously, you watch yourself feeling, the feeling will lose its integrity and become a cerebral invention: you will no longer know what you really feel, and you will finally feel very little, if anything. You will have lost your sincerity. Hampshire, on the other hand, thinks that the ideal of naturalness of feeling, uncorrupted by reflection, is undesirable as well as unattainable—unattainable largely by reason of the "peculiarities of reflexive knowledge, that is, of the knowledge that a man has of his own contemporary intentional states." Sincerity is a congruence between what a person is disposed to say about himself—his

---

31. Conrad, *Under Western Eyes,* Introduction by Morton D. Zabel (New York: New Classics Series, 1951), 279. Herbert Read, "Swift," in *The Nature of Literature* (New York: Horizon 1956; originally published in 1938 as *Collected Essays in Literary Criticism*), 208. Read later changed his mind in part: "All art is artifice, and therefore no work of art is sincere." "The Cult of Sincerity," in *The Cult of Sincerity* (London: Faber and Faber, 1968), 18.

attitudes or sentiments—and what he is disposed to do. Identifying what one thinks or feels or wants, however, is not like identifying physical objects. People may be—often are—confused about their subjective lives: they may cling sincerely to incompatible propositions or to incompatible attitudes toward a given event. "Descriptions of states of mind, of beliefs, desires, and emotions," says Hampshire, "are liable to a kind of indeterminacy which has no parallel in description of physical states."[32]

Hampshire mentions briefly the influence that surpressed or less than conscious ideas may have on such description, but he does not bring up the immense challenge to the concept of sincerity posed by the Freudian description of man. Psychoanalysis has shown that a desire or a passion can emerge in completely inverted form: "A work can be the very fantasy which compensates the negative life: Oreste in love with Hermione," writes Roland Barthes, "is perhaps Racine secretly disgusted with Mlle Duparc." As for the difficulty of the sincere man who sincerely tries to be sincere, a longer quotation from Hampshire will be instructive:

> A natural feeling, which is also a strong and sincere feeling, is a passion; and the ethics of romanticism represents the man of passion as the ideal of the sincere man of undivided mind. But the ethics of romanticism only with difficulty avoids contradiction and turns very easily into an attitude of irony, as Stendhal showed; for the cultivation of strong and sincere passions, as a policy—"espagnolisme," as Stendhal called it—requires either a restraint of intelligence, or a kind of self-consciousness that amounts to sentimentality. How can a man watch for, and endorse, his own moments of spontaneity and natural passion without an ironical awareness of his own duplicity?

32. Jean-Paul Sartre, *Existential Psychoanalysis* [from *Being and Nothingness*], trans. Hazel E. Barnes (New York: Philosophical Library, 1953), 248. Stuart Hampshire, "Sincerity and Single-Mindedness," in *Freedom of Mind and Other Essays* (Princeton: Princeton University Press, 1971), 232–56.

Hampshire's answer to his own question is much to our purpose. "The answer is that he can do this only in fiction, by creating a representative of himself." In the interests of a genuine sincerity, that is, the writer must create a persona. Artifice is as natural to man as spontaneity. Here irony and paradox enter the domain of sincerity in a way that Conrad's Sophia Antonovna could hardly have imagined.[33]

33. Roland Barthes, "The Two Criticisms," in *Critical Essays,* trans. Richard Howard (Evanston, Ill.: Northwestern University Press, 1972), 252. Hampshire, 250.

4 The Question of Truth

The Lies of Fiction and
the Truths of History

The historian, says Sir Philip Sidney, is "captived to the truth of a foolish world," whereas the poet has "all, from Dante's heaven to his hell, under the authority of his pen." A basic principle for the Renaissance, the ancient opposition between poetry and history, today is rapidly breaking down as writers on each side of the division constituted by the idea of truth test the limits of their respective modes. To be sure, it has always been recognized that neither mode is pure: dramatists and writers of fiction have from the beginning felt free to incorporate historical figures into their work, and Sidney acknowledges that historians since Herodotus have put orations into the mouths of kings that the kings certainly never uttered. The deliberate, self-conscious effort to dissolve boundaries, however, is largely a twentieth-century phenomenon. Truman Capote's "nonfiction novel" *In Cold Blood* (1965), by calling into question normally accepted categories, stimulated many similar explorations. A distinguished example is Norman Mailer's *The Executioner's Song* (1979). Mailer describes the work as a "factual account" of the career of the executed murderer Gary Gilmore—this "dare I say it, *true life* story, with its real names and real lives." Mailer adds that he presents the story "as if it were a novel." The Library of Congress classifies *The Executioner's Song* as fiction, and of course it was in the fiction category that it won the Pulitzer Prize in 1980.[1]

On the other side of the division Robert Woodward and Scott Armstrong in *The Brethren* (1979), a historical study of the United States Supreme Court under Chief Justice Burger, make up dialogue and purport to give us the thoughts of the justices as though they were fictional characters. The procedure violates one of the most fundamental principles of serious historical writing.

In addition to subversive explorations such as these the presumed radical opposition between history and fiction has been brought under brilliant theoretical attack by the philosophical historian Hayden White. According to White, the events of history are value-free in themselves and take on value only when they are organized into a particular kind of story. A decision by the historian as to whether the story he tells is tragic or comic, romantic or ironic, governs the innumerable choices he must make about the details constituting his enterprise, choices about whether to select a detail or suppress it, highlight it or frame it or relegate it to background. The historian is like a novelist or playwright in these matters as he struggles to organize his materials, his decisions significantly governed by the genre in which he is working. For example, the events of the French Revolution—roughly the same events for each historian—constitute a tragic story or an ironic one, according to the organizational disposition of the historian, according, that is, to the generic decision he has made. Historical narratives, writes White, are "verbal fictions, the contents of which are as much

---

1. Sir Philip Sidney, *An Apology for Poetry,* ed. Geoffrey Shepherd (London: Nelson, 1965), 111, 97; Norman Mailer, *The Executioner's Song* (Boston: Little, Brown, 1979), 1053. Mailer's earlier *Armies of the Night* (1968) has as subtitle *History as a Novel: The Novel as History.*

invented as *found* and the forms of which have more in common with their counterparts in literature than they have with those of the sciences."[2]

White's thesis could hardly be more controversial. Since Aristotle, history has purported to tell the truth about the world, above all the factual truth, whereas the poets have been gloriously, and scandalously, free from such constraints. Free from their own point of view, that is; not from that of others. Plato's charge against them has appeared in many forms, never more vehemently than in the attacks of certain sixteenth-century Protestant sects on poets as liars. Thomas More's assertion that the Protestant reformer Richard Hunne had not been murdered by his jailers, as was claimed, but had in fact committed suicide, was contemptuously dismissed by William Tyndale and his colleagues on the grounds that More was a notorious liar. Their proof? Any man who would pass off the lies of *Utopia* as truth would not hesitate to lie any time it suited his purpose. Similarly, in theological argument More's defense of the existence of Purgatory was taken by the reformers to be exactly on a level with his description of Utopia: one was as imaginary as the other, and More lied by claiming either existed.[3]

Such literalness is of course extreme, but in the Middle Ages and Renaissance fiction's bad conscience with respect to truth may be seen in the elaborate efforts of writers to provide documentation establishing the "authenticity" of their tales. The imagination was known and valued as a source of delight, but it was recognized also to be the faculty that distorted and falsified reality: hence all the circumstantiality of diaries, letters, found manuscripts—frame devices of all sorts—employed to anchor

2. Hayden White, "The Historical Text as Literary Artifact," *Clio* 3 (1974): 277–304; reprinted in *Tropics of Discourse* (Baltimore: Johns Hopkins University Press, 1978), 81–100. White's thesis is developed at length in his *Metahistory: The Historical Imagination in Nineteenth Century Europe* (Baltimore: Johns Hopkins University Press, 1973).

3. See Rainer Pineas, "Thomas More's *Utopia* and Protestant Polemics," *Renaissance News* 17 (1964): 197–201.

made-up stories into the real world. Cervantes plays lovely games with the problem, but for many of his successors, Samuel Richardson, for example, it is a critical matter. Bishop Warburton, out of his admiration for Richardson, proffered a preface to *Clarissa Harlowe* which said straight out that the story of Clarissa is fiction, the letters made up. Reluctant to offend the bishop, Richardson was intensely embarrassed as he sought to square his moral purpose as a novelist with the question of historical truth. He wrote to Warburton:

> Will you, good Sir, allow me to mention, that I could wish that the *Air* of Genuineness had been kept up, tho' I want not the Letters to be *thought* genuine; only so far kept up, I mean, as that they should not prefatically be owned *not* to be genuine: and this for fear of weakening their Influence where any of them are aimed to be exemplary; as well as to avoid hurting that kind of Historical Faith which Fiction itself is generally read with, tho' we know it to be Fiction.[4]

The "Air of Genuineness" is of course what poets and writers of fiction have always aimed at, cultivating elaborate forms of deception in the process. Poets try to give an air of truthfulness to their fictions, says David Hume, but in fact they are liars by profession. More recent philosophers are likely to abstain from the bare epithet, but the question of truth still embarrasses. A work of literary art, says A. J. Ayer, is constituted by propositions that are all literally false; but the work need not, he grants, be the worse for that. A novel for Gilbert Ryle is full of "pseudo-propositions": propositions about Mr. Pickwick cannot be true or false, for (as far as we know) there was no such person as Mr. Pickwick. Hence the propositions of fiction—at least those of the kind containing the pseudo-designation "Mr. Pickwick"—are not really about anything at all. Even when

---

4. See Morton W. Bloomfield, "Authenticating Realism and the Realism of Chaucer," *Thought* 39 (1964): 335–68; William Nelson, *Fact or Fiction: The Dilemma of the Renaissance Storyteller* (Cambridge, Mass.: Harvard University Press, 1973), throughout. The Richardson example is in Nelson, 111–12.

novels contain examples of social or psychological truths, insofar as the truths have to do with imaginary characters, the propositions expressing those truths and professing to be about the characters are fictions. G. E. Moore in the same symposium disagrees with Ryle, at least in part, on the matter of pseudo-propositions. He thinks the words "That proposition of Dickens' was about Mr. Pickwick" express a true proposition, whereas Ryle would say the proposition is neither true nor false.[5]

The controversy over the persona is one phase of this large and venerable debate. Those critics who most strongly oppose the idea of the persona tend to take the position that unless obvious signals in a poem indicate irony or an attempt to deceive, readers are obligated to accept an author's statements in his work at face value. Specifically, when an author writing in the first person makes an assertion about himself, and signals no disclaimers, he is claiming to tell the truth and should be believed. Irvin Ehrenpreis, for example, objects to persona criticism because, he says, it substitutes an impersonal speaker for the poet and thus severs the connection of the poem with history and historical truth. If the purpose of the poem is to *appear* truthful rather than to be truthful, then the rhetorical device of the persona may, he grants, be called for; but Ehrenpreis has little use for this kind of rhetoric:

> As audience, we try to discover what the real author [as opposed to the persona] means in the particular work.... At the moment, in the poem, he says what we have to accept as his assertion if no evidence appears to the contrary.... So long as there is no hint of deceitfulness, what a man says must be precisely what he means. In suggesting that we are not to

5. David Hume, *Treatise of Human Nature,* bk.1, pt. 3, sec. 10; ed. L. A. Selby-Bigge (Oxford: Oxford University Press, 1928), 121; A. J. Ayer, *Language, Truth and Logic* (London: Victor Gollancz, 1962), 44–45; Gilbert Ryle, "Imaginary Objects," in *Creativity, Politics and the A Priori,* The Aristotelian Society, supplementary vol. 12 (London: Harrison, 1933), 26–27; G. E. Moore, ibid., 59.

take Pope at his word when he makes a statement in a poem, an essay, or a private letter, the critic is turning a genius into a fool."[6]

Such approaches to autobiographical statements in poems or in other literary modes lead, I think, to sterilities of the kind we encountered in the interpretation of Robert Lowell's "Skunk Hour." Say, for example, we identify the speaker of "The Epistle to Dr. Arbuthnot" unequivocally with Alexander Pope and accept that he means precisely what he says, as Ehrenpreis wants us to do. Under those rules we are bound to test any claim about himself made in the poem by our understanding of the life and character of the historical Alexander Pope. At several points in the poem the speaker expresses his abhorrence of falsehood:

how wretched I!
Who can't be silent, and who will not lie. (lines 33–34)

Or, again, the speaker claims that when his poems were unjustifiably criticized, he merely smiled; when the criticism was just, "I kissed the rod" (line 158). We know that Pope lied to friend and enemy alike in his complex literary dealings, and we know that with critics he was much more likely to wield the rod than to kiss it. Applying Ehrenpreis's criteria, we conclude that Pope lies about lying in the poem and that he lies about his relations with critics. The conclusion seems to me decidedly uninteresting, nor is it one with which it is possible to be satisfied. If we apply those standards to the statements of poets in their poems, who shall 'scape whipping?[7]

---

6. Ehrenpreis, "Personae," in *Literary Meaning and Augustan Values,* 51–52; cf. his "Explicitness in Augustan Literature," ibid., 1–48.
7. See Donald Greene in the Persona symposium, *Satire News Letter,* Spring 1966), 119.

Autobiography and
Autobiographical Fiction
and Poetry

"To speak in the first person," writes Elizabeth Bruss, "is to identify oneself as the immediate source of the communication, and to make of this a focal issue of that communication." The general context of Bruss's statement is autobiography, but its truth applies far beyond that to nonliterary as well as literary discourse, with a few obvious exceptions in both categories. Within literature, for example, it is accepted that characters in drama speaking in the first person speak for themselves, not (or not directly) for their creator, although even that convention is sometimes challenged. Jeremy Collier insisted " 'tis the Poet that speaks in the *Persons* of the Stage" and that when a character utters "Smut and Profaneness" in a play, the playwright's *"private Sentiments* fall under Censure." The first person sentiments of Dogberry or Iago are rarely attributed to Shakespeare, but the same cannot be said of statements by Hamlet or Timon or Prospero. Again, to adopt Robert Langbaum's distinction, the dramatic monologue (Browning's "My Last Duchess," Tennyson's "Ulysses") is an obvious exception to Bruss's statement, the dramatic lyric (Keats's "Ode to a Nightingale") is not. Characters in novels speak in their own persons, we say, and with their own voices—when, that is, they are obviously distinct from the author; but first person narrators of novels are often problematic.[8]

More obviously than with any other genre, however, it is in autobiography that the first person becomes the focal issue of communication. A constitutive rule of the genre is that the autobiographer's report makes a claim on truth. For obvious reasons, the claim is often challenged, prompting writers to offer

8. Elizabeth Bruss, *Autobiographical Acts* (Baltimore: Johns Hopkins University Press, 1976), 21; Jeremy Collier, "Defence of the Short View," cited in Aubrey Williams, "No Cloistered Virtue: or Playwright vs. Priest in 1698," *PMLA* 90 (1975): 239.

warranties for the truths they profess. Jean Starobinski points out that the unassailable warrant for the truth of St. Augustine's *Confessions* is the fact that they are addressed to God. To be sure, God, who is omniscient and knows the inmost secrets of Augustine's heart—the secrets of every heart from the beginning of time—has no need of Augustine's written account; but his presence as interlocutor guarantees the commitment to veracity. How could Augustine lie to God? The secondary adressee of the *Confessions*—Augustine's readers—are the ones who really need the story and for whose sake it is elaborated. Their edification is the motive.[9]

In contrast, Rousseau's *Confessions,* Starobinski shows, enjoy a much less firm guarantee of truth, for Rousseau's relations with God are on a different plane from those of Augustine. True, Rousseau invokes God at the beginning of the *Confessions* and promises that on Judgment Day he will appear before the Throne, book in hand, to assert its truthfulness. From this point on, however, God nearly disappears from the work. Replacing him, the principal warrant for the writer's truth, is Rousseau's strenuously invoked sincerity. The difference in value between the two warrants, the cultural gap between them, is immense.[10]

No matter how committed the autobiographer may be to historical truth he will be obliged to acknowledge, if he is honest, how elusive that truth is. "I have changed nothing [in the account of my life] to my knowledge," writes Yeats, "and yet it must be that I have changed many things without my knowledge." Francis R. Hart says in a fine essay on the subject that problems about the relation of the fictive to the historical in autobiography, *Dichtung und Wahrheit,* are, though inescapable, in some degree pseudo-problems. So closely intertwined are the two seemingly antithetical stands in the writing of one's life, anyone's life, that to separate them is impossible. As Yeats

9. Jean Starobinski, "The Style of Autobiography," trans. Seymour Chatman, in James Olney, ed., *Autobiography* (Princeton: Princeton University Press, 1980), 77–78.

10. Starobinski, 80–81.

suggests, it is not as though the "I" who writes about himself deliberately falsifies matters (although that of course happens too), but in addition to the failures and confusions of memory there is the infinitely complex process of deciding what from a lifetime's experience is to be included, what left out, what and whom and where and when to be emphasized, what subordinated. Any organization of a life story resulting from those choices must be in some degree fictitious. Valéry says that every confession, every memoir, is a confession of someone "more impressive, purer, blacker, livelier... and even more himself than is permissible, for self has its degrees."[11]

Today, an influential group of contemporary French writers deny the existence of the self entirely; but, undeterred, they still write autobiographies of sorts, making literature out of the paradoxes involved. The text of *Roland Barthes by Roland Barthes,* written by Roland Barthes and then reviewed by him, is preceded by the statement: "It must all be considered as though spoken by a character in a novel." Other sophisticated autobiographers like Nabokov give ambiguous signals about the historicity of their accounts, although Nabokov claims in *Speak, Memory* that the man in him is in revolt against the fictionist. But in the nature of things the fictionist is there, not free as he is in the novel to follow his story where the logic of the imagination leads, constrained by the facts in the case, but he is there nevertheless. It is certainly not as bad as Freud said: "What makes all autobiographies worthless is, after all, their mendacity"; for in the great examples the mendacity has been metamorphosed into art. The autobiographer may not express the historical truth as exactly as the pure historian might wish, but he may in compensation create another kind of truth of transcendent validity. He may, indeed, in the act of writing, create as well as discover a self. Valéry was fond of saying that just as

11. William Butler Yeats, Preface to the *Autobiography* (New York: Macmillan, 1953), 2; Francis R. Hart, "Notes for an Anatomy of Modern Autobiography," in *New Directions in Literary History,* ed. Ralph Cohen (Baltimore: Johns Hopkins University Press, 1974), 221ff.; Paul Valéry, "Stendhal," in *Masters and Friends,* 197.

a criminal may be the product of his crime, so a writer may be "created" by what he writes of himself.[12]

A subgenre of ambiguously autobiographical works play adroitly against the history-fiction complication in autobiography proper, toying with our uncertainty about what kind of truth the reader may expect. Christopher Isherwood, for one, has been highly successful at exploiting these uncertainties. In an early account of his youth, *Lions and Shadows: an Education in the Twenties* (1938), Isherwood nearly disclaims the title autobiography altogether. He announces in a foreword to the reader that the book contains no revelations, is not indiscreet: "it is not even entirely 'true.'" Read it as a novel, Isherwood counsels, for he has used a novelist's license in relating incidents, and his characters from life are given fictitious names. (Even these disguises are meant to be at least partially permeable: for example, Wystan Hugh Auden is called Hugh Weston.) If the autobiography *Lions and Shadows* reads like a novel, Isherwood's novels read very like autobiography. The protagonist in a series of them is called Christopher Isherwood, whose progress in searching out his own identity casts him into a close but complex relationship with the author of the same name. For example, *Down There on a Visit* (1962) starts as a conventional novel written in the first person: "In the spring of 1928, when I was twenty-three years old, Mr. Lancaster came to London." The narration quickly halts, however, for comment: "And now before I slip back into the convention of calling this young man 'I,' let me consider him as a separate being." The two "I's" may indeed share the same skeleton and have in common the label of their name and a continuity of consciousness; nevertheless, they are almost strangers, so much has Isherwood the author revised the young Christopher's opinions, mannerisms, and prejudices—so much has he himself changed in the intervening years. Strangers or no, however, "there has been no break in the sequence of daily statements that I am I." And Isherwood owes Christopher

12. Sigmund Freud in a letter to Edward L. Bernays: *Letters*, trans. Tania and James Stern (New York: Basic Books, 1960), 391.

respect: "In a sense he is my Father, and in another sense my son." [13]

Many readers accepted the portrait of the persona Christopher as on the whole a full and faithful depiction of his creator. How inadequate that indentification is has become clear with the later novels and the recent autobiographical work *Christopher and His Kind* (1976). In the stories about the Berlin of the 1930s *(Goodbye to Berlin, The Last of Mr. Norris)* the narrator is presented as an essentially passive figure, emotionally aloof from the bizarre life surrounding him, emotionally uninvolved in the frenetic sexual goings-on characteristic of the time: John Van Druten's dramatic version of the stories, *I Am a Camera,* has made the "objectivity" famous. How far from actuality it was *Christopher and His Kind* makes clear (Isherwood still writes in the first person of Christopher in the third).

> Christopher's first visit to Berlin [described in innocuous terms in *Down There on a Visit*] was short—a week or ten days—but that was sufficient; I now recognize it as one of the decisive events of my life. I can still make myself faintly feel the delicious nausea of initiation terror which Christopher felt as Wystan pushed back the heavy leather door curtain of a boy bar called the Cosy Corner and led the way inside. [14]

The decision not to make the narrator of the novels (in most cases, Christopher) identical in character and personality with Isherwood had behind it both social and artistic motives. For one thing, Isherwood confesses in *Christopher and His Kind* that he was afraid of the scandal that would have ensued if he had made Christopher into an overt homosexual. The principal artistic reason was that in *The Last of Mr. Norris,* for example, he wanted the reader's attention focused on Mr. Norris, not on the narrator. The reader was to be encouraged to see with the narrator's eyes, to identify with him; but, writes Isherwood, if Christopher

13. Christopher Isherwood, *Down There on a Visit* (London: Methuen, 1962), 12–14.

14. Christopher Isherwood, *Christopher and His Kind* (New York: Farrar, Straus and Giroux, 1976), 3.

had made his narrator (William Bradshaw in this case, but the change of name is purely formal) an avowed homosexual, with a homosexual's attitudes and prejudices, there would be the danger that for many readers the narrator's oddity, perhaps his interest, would shunt aside Mr. Norris as the center of attention. As for making the narrator a heterosexual, says Isherwood, Christopher scorned to do that. Here the constraints of history clearly limit the imaginative possibilities of the work.

Christopher and His Kind has a special kind of interest as it attempts to unravel the ambiguous relations of fiction and autobiography which Isherwood has so skillfully manipulated in his work. "The book I am now going to write," says Isherwood in the Preface, "will be as frank and factual as I can make it, especially as far as I myself am concerned." Reading *Christopher,* says Gabriele Annan, is like watching a man take out his own appendix, and there is no question but that the book is written close to the bone. A political act of major significance to the author, the confession of homosexuality energizes the book and provides insight into an aspect of his character that Isherwood considers central to his whole being—an aspect that novelistic autobiography and autobiographical novels had left unexplored. Here, surely, we must feel, is a truthful portrait, the narrator's rendering of Christopher—and of himself as he writes of Christopher—altogether accurate. Doubtless the portrait is true in the way of such things; but, schooled by Mr. Isherwood, a careful reader is likely to be on the lookout—and to be listening—for an I behind the "I" of Mr. Isherwood's presentation.

Proust's situation is not dissimilar, although he wrote no *Christopher and His Kind* and always maintained vehemently that the "je" of *A la recherche du temps perdu* was not he. As Michel Butor says, Proust insists that the "'je' est un autre, et il nous donne comme argument péremptoire: 'c'est un roman.'" To me it seems a good argument. Roger Shattuck speaks of a fission-fusion process in Proust's management of the first person singular: he combines the awkwardly-disposed third person of *Jean Santeuil* with his various early uses of the first person to form the

"I" of *Remembrance of Things Past*–a narrator and a character in one pronoun; and at the same time he divides himself, his life, his character, among Charlus, Swann, Bloch, as well as Marcel and the narrator. Between the authorial voice and that of the narrator, who is given the name Marcel, there is no obvious ironic distance. Thus we are invited to make the identification even as Proust disclaims it.[15]

At one point in the last book there occurs a passage in which the identification between Proust and Marcel seems fleetingly to become unmistakable. Suddenly, under the strain of great emotion, the conventions of novelistic discourse are dropped; Proust seems to speak in his own person, to make a claim on the reality outside the fictional realm of the book. The narrator is speaking of the dreadful period of the first World War. In a paroxysm of patriotic fervor he does honor to the millionaires who, when a nephew was killed, ran his café and refused to take a sou in payment.

In this book in which there is not a single incident which is not fictitious, not a single character who is a real person in disguise, in which everything has been invented by me in accordance with the requirements of my theme, I owe it to the credit of my country to say that only the millionaire cousins of Françoise who came out of retirement to help their niece when she was left without support, only they are real people who exist. And persuaded as I am that I shall not offend their modesty, for the reason that they will never read this book, it is both with childish pleasure and with a profound emotion that, being unable to record the names of so many others who undoubtedly acted in the same way, to all of whom France owes her survival, I transcribe here the real name of this family . . . Larivière.[16]

15. Michel Butor, "L'Usage des pronoms personnels dans le roman," *Répertoire II* (Paris: Editions de Minuit, 1964), 61; Roger Shattuck, *Proust* (London: Fontana Modern Masters, 1974), 26.

16. Proust, *The Past Recaptured,* trans. Andreas Mayor (New York: Random House, 1970), 113. The French text: "Dans ce livre où il n'y a pas un seul fait qui ne soit fictif, où il n'y a pas un seul personnage 'à clefs,' où tout a été inventé par

How does one read it? Within a single sentence the fictional and the historical confront each other in unresolved and vertiginous contradiction. Who is the *moi* who has invented the whole mammoth work? Is this Marcel claiming that the past he has reconstructed with such tenacity, such delicacy, with such apparent fidelity, is not in fact his own past but one he has created for *his* novel? Can it be Marcel who bangs the table in a passion of patriotism and says: Françoise's cousins are real people, they live in the real world, they behaved splendidly, their name is Larivière? Or is Proust causing his persona to play ontological games with his readers, testing (like a Pirandello in the drama) how far the limits of fiction can be stretched by the claim: this is not fiction? I am not a Proust scholar and have no special competence here, but I do not think we are to read this passage as though Marcel is being "consciously" paradoxical. To my ear, this is Proust speaking, violating the conventions of fiction, for the moment incorporating Marcel wholly into himself, making a truth claim on the real world: "I transcribe here the real name of this family . . . Larivière." It is a strange moment in the huge, superbly controlled work, in formal terms very like a climactic moment in Jonathan Swift's *A Tale of a Tub,* to be discussed in chapter six. Is it an error? But what would it mean to label "error" a shift in voice which makes possible a passage of such remarkable power?

One would think that poetry written in the first person would be more sheltered than prose from questions of historical truth, simply by reason of its more obvious stylization and the strength of the convention: the poet nothing affirmeth. On the other

---

moi selon les besoins de ma démonstration, je dois dire à la louange de mon pays que seuls les parents millionnaires de Françoise ayant quitté leur retraite pour aider leur nièce sans appui, que seuls ceux-là sont des gens réels, qui existent. Et persuadé que leur modestie ne s'en offensera pas, pour la raison qu'ils ne liront jamais ce livre, c'est avec un enfantin plaisir et une profonde émotion que, ne pouvant citer les noms de tant d'autres qui durent agir de même et mar qui la France a survécu, je transcris ici leur nom véritable: ils s'appellent . . . Larivière." *A la recherce du temps perdu,* ed. Pierre Clarac and André Ferré, 3 vols. (Paris: Gallimard, 1954), 3:846. Shattuck calls attention to this passage.

hand, like the novelist the poet may cultivate an air of truth with such success that the context markers are ignored and his poetic statements made captive to the truth of a foolish world. One of a thousand possible examples would be Wordsworth's poem "The Last of the Flock," one of the *Lyrical Ballads,* a pathetic dialogue between the first person speaker and a shepherd whom poverty has forced to sell off his sheep one by one. A critic in the *Monthly Review* offered this admonition: "If the author be a wealthy man, he ought not to have suffered this poor peasant to part with the last of the flock." The critic's assumption that the dialogue of the poem is a versified transcription of reality is perfectly understandable, a natural consequence of the air of reality which Wordsworth cultivates.[17]

On the other hand, the poet himself may be uneasy about the status of factual claims made in a poem. In another one of the *Lyrical Ballads* Wordsworth describes a lonesome peak off to the west:

> one of these our hills . . .
> We can behold it from our Orchard-seat.

Years later, struck apparently by qualms about the truth of the statement, Wordsworth says in the Fenwick note to the poem: "It is not accurate that the Eminence here alluded to could be seen from our orchard-seat. It rises above the road by the side of Grasmere lake, towards Keswick, and its name is Stone-Arthur." The schoolmaster he has described in another one of the *Lyrical Ballads* is, he admits, a composite figure, like the Wanderer in the *Excursion:* "I do not ask pardon for what there is of untruth in such verses, considered strictly as matters of fact." They are, he says, true in spirit. Wordsworth's defiant refusal to apologize shows plainly how uncomfortable he was with the convention which makes conformity to matters of fact in poetry unnecessary and often undesirable. It ran athwart his convictions about sincerity, for one thing, and raised questions about

17. See David Perkins, *Wordsworth and the Poetry of Sincerity* (Cambridge, Mass.: Harvard University Press, 1964), 35ff.

different kinds of truth that a man of his temperament could hardly be easy with.[18]

Much of the appeal of the *Prelude,* which Wordsworth calls a history of his own mind, is attributable to the air of authenticity in the poem; the poet, we feel, is singleheartedly intent on telling the truth about himself. As readers we in effect overhear "meditations in the Author's own person," as Wordsworth calls them, meditations addressed to Coleridge:

> I speak bare truth,
> As if to thee alone in private talk.
>
> (1805, 10, 372–73)

Given Wordsworth's concern for the bare truth, it comes as a surprise to learn that, like other poets, he writes autobiographical poems based very little on his own experience, and he sometimes manipulates that experience as a novelist would. Consider "Resolution and Independence," the famous poem in which the speaker is shamed out of a mood of black melancholy by the Leech Gatherer, the ancient man who in his decrepitude wanders the lonely moors following his trade, an unforgettable example of courage and steadfastness:

> He told, that to these waters he had come
> To gather leeches, being old and poor:
> Employment hazardous and wearisome!
> And he had many hardships to endure:
> From pond to pond he roamed, from moor
>   to moor;
> Housing, with God's good help, by choice or
>   chance;
> and in this way he gained an honest maintenance.

Sara Hutchinson saw the poem in manuscript and made some mild criticism. In a letter to Sara, Wordsworth passionately defends the poem.

---

18. William Wordsworth, *Poetical Works,* ed. Ernest de Selincourt and Helen Darbishire, 5 vols. (Oxford: Oxford University Press, 1949–58), 2:488; 4:415.

I will explain to you in prose my feeling in writing that Poem.... I describe myself as having been exalted to the highest pitch of delight by the joyousness and beauty of Nature and then as depressed, even in the midst of those beautiful objects, to the lowest dejection and despair. A young Poet in the midst of the happiness of Nature is described as overwhelmed by the thought of the miserable reverses which have befallen the happiest of all men, viz Poets—I think of this till I am so deeply impressed by it, that I consider the manner in which I was rescued from my dejection and despair almost as an interposition of Providence.... A person reading this Poem with feelings like mine will have been awed and controuled, expecting almost something spiritual or supernatural—What is brought forward? "A lonely place, a Pond" "by which an old man *was,* far from all house or home"—not stood, not sat, but "was."... But Good God! Such a figure, in such a place, a pious self-respecting, miserably infirm, and [   ] Old Man telling such a tale![19]

By that repeated and emphasized "was" Wordsworth insists upon the substantiality of the scene, its reality as epiphany. From his sister Dorothy's *Journal,* however, we learn that she and Wordsworth met the old man, not on the lonely moor but on the highway. He had given up gathering leeches, which had become scarce. "He lived by begging," Dorothy recorded, "and was making his way to Carlisle, where he should buy a few godly books to sell." Thus the vividly imaged scene—the old man bent over double, stirring the muddy pond with his staff—a splendid example of Robert Langbaum's poetry of experience—comes not from direct physical experience itself but from the imagination. So intensely imagined is the scene that Wordsworth, speaking of himself both in the first and third persons in the letter, almost claims for it historical reality. The letter comes much closer to making a false statement than does the poem because of the form of discourse employed.[20]

19. *The Letters of William and Dorothy Wordsworth,* ed. Ernest de Selincourt, rev. Chester L. Shaver, 2d ed., 3 vols. (Oxford: Clarendon, 1967), 1:366–67.
20. Dorothy Wordsworth, *Journals,* ed. Ernest de Selincourt, 2 vols. (New York: Macmillan, 1941), 1:63. Frederick A. Pottle discusses Wordsworth's

But the question of factual truth should not rise for the poem at all. The speaker, who certainly in some major sense represents William Wordsworth, claims to have had an experience that we know from history Wordsworth did not have. (Dorothy's *Journal* must be considered a more reliable historical source than Wordsworth's letter or poem.) To make this contradiction an issue, however, it is to assume that the identification between the "I" of the poem and the historical person of the poet is unequivocal. Given the nature of language, however, and given the conventions governing literary discourse, equivocation in identifications of that kind is necessary.

Readers who are disturbed over discrepancies between statements in poems and the facts of the case in the real world are caught up in a false dilemma. St. Augustine presents the operative principle magnificently:

> On the stage [the actor] Roscius was a false Hecuba by choice, a true man by nature; but by that choice also a true tragic actor because he fulfilled his purpose, yet a false Priam because he imitated Priam but was not he. And now from this comes something amazing, which however no one doubts . . . that all these things are true in some respects . . . and that only the fact that they are false in one sense helps them towards their truth. Hence they cannot in any way arrive where they would be or should be if they shrink from being false. For how could the actor I mentioned be a true tragic actor if he were not willing to be a false Hector, a false Andromache, a false Hercules . . . ? Or how could a picture of a horse be a true picture unless it were a false horse? or an image of a man in a mirror be a true image unless it were a false man? So if the fact that they are false in one respect helps certain things to be true in another respect, why do we fear falseness so much and seek truth as such a great good? . . . Will we not admit that these things make up truth itself, that truth is so to speak put together from them?[21]

manipulation of his experience in "The Eye and the Object in the Poetry of Wordsworth," in *Wordsworth: Centenary Essays,* ed. Gilbert T. Dunklin (Princeton: Princeton University Press, 1951), 23–42.

21. St. Augustine, *Soliloquia,* 2.10, trans. Donald R. Howard and Georg Luck,

The supreme example within the Christian tradition of truth achieved by a "false" actor is doubtless Dante's *Divine Comedy*. As Charles Singleton says, the fiction of the *Divine Comedy* is that it is not a fiction. Nowhere in the poem is this detailed representation of the state of souls after death presented as though it were a vision or a dream, according to the familiar medieval model. Dante presents himself, in the first person, as the flesh-and-blood poet who experiences, and then records, what the poem describes. Like St. Augustine's actor Roscius, he is a false (better "fictive") pilgrim whose fictive character is essential to the kind of truth that the poem achieves. Plato distinguishes in the *Republic* between two kinds of falsehood: the true falsehood in the soul about the nature of reality—an abomination; and a spoken falsehood which may be helpful, an embodiment of truth. The poet who would use the latter kind of falsehood (or fiction) must himself know the truth. If the *Republic* had been Christian and medieval, Charles Singleton says, Plato would not have banished Dante from it. Dante, he says, was Plato's poet.[22]

From Poetry to Life

It is dishonest of us as critics, writes Donald Davie, to use the concept of the persona as a way of interpreting those autobiographical poems in which the writers are clearly trying to cut loose from what he calls the nets of rhetoric, trying to break out into the world of truth. Why do we refuse to recognize this? Davie asks. "Why is it so important to us as critics to seal off the world of literature from the adjacent worlds of biography and history and geography? What are we afraid of?"[23]

As the history of the twentieth century shows with relentless clarity, boundaries in art—all the arts—exist in order to

in Howard, *The Idea of the Canterbury Tales* (Berkeley: University of California Press, 1976), 196.

22. Charles S. Singleton, *Dante Studies, I, Commedia: Elements of Structure* (Cambridge, Mass.: Harvard University Press, 1954), 62, 70; Plato, *Republic*, 2:382.

23. Donald Davie, "On Sincerity," *Encounter*, October 1968, 65.

be broken: the defining artistic gesture of our age is that which calls into question the status of art itself. What are we afraid of? We might well be afraid of what happens when the barriers between rhetoric and everyday reality are thrown over. Instructive examples are in large supply.

According to Julian Beck, the Living Theatre was started with the intention of doing away with barriers, changing the form of theatrical presentation itself. Early plays of the Living Theatre were of the kind that pretend not to be plays at all—the actors feigning they are rehearsing a play, or getting ready to make a movie, as with Pirandello or Jack Gelber's *The Connection*. The purpose here was to disrupt normal assumptions about the relation between actors and audience, between actors' space and "real" space; to destroy the frame which establishes a privileged ontological mode for the world on stage. The group comprising the Living Theatre, however, who are committed anarchists and intent on speaking the truth, became uneasy with this sophisticated theatrical mode. They decided that what they were projecting in the theater was fundamentally false, a violation of their anarchist principles: "we felt that you really can't lie to an audience that way." Judith Malina, a cofounder, elaborates:

> That is, it compounds the fiction in a very strange way. If I say "I'm Hedda Gabler and I've had a very unhappy life," that's one kind of lie; but if I say, "Now, I am not speaking as Hedda Gabler, now I am speaking as Judith Malina" and I am saying somebody else's words written for me, then it's a much worse lie than to say, "I am Hedda Gabler," because I've compounded the distance between myself and the spectator.[24]

"Are you really Robert Young?" asks the actor in the television commercial. "Yes, I am," the real Robert Young replies. "So you really do drink Sanka brand!" "Yes, I love it." Young's "reality" and all those "really's" are an effort to blur the distinction between rhetoric and reality, and, of course, to sell coffee.

---

24. Judith Malina and Julian Beck, interviewed by Richard Schechner, *Tulane Drama Review* 13 (Spring 1969): 37. I have altered the punctuation somewhat.

Beck and Malina want to destroy the distinction. They want a society in which one can believe Robert Young.

The culmination of the Living Theatre's efforts to break out of the nets of rhetoric was *Paradise Now,* a semi-improvisational piece in which all distinction between actors and audience is obliterated. Deliberately destroying the otherness of art in a rite of total participation, shedding their clothes in "primitivistic" abandon, the undifferentiated participants—all actors now in an untheatrical sense—take to the streets in pursuit of an evanescent reality. With *Paradise Now,* says Julian Beck, the Living Theatre "wanted to make a play which would no longer be an enactment but would be the act itself."[25]

But programmatic truth-telling brings its own dilemmas. If it is lying to speak in the person of Hedda Gabbler, is it telling the truth to say to members of an audience that you love them, and offer as surety the intimacy of naked bodies? Stefan Brecht criticizes *Paradise Now* because the actors manipulate the feelings of the audience, pretending to a sincere intimacy they do not in fact feel. Eric Bentley condemns the gestures of love as unreal. The ways of sincerity, as we observed in the preceding chapter, are treacherous.[26]

In another move to shatter the frame that sets off theater from life, one producer put a family on stage in Greenwich Village, instructed them to live normally in this unorthodox domestic space, and collected money for tickets. Such efforts to fuse art and reality are unhandsome reflections of certain utopian specu-lations about the status of art in a putative good society of the future. Herbert Marcuse, for example, envisaged a society in which "technique would tend to become art and art would tend to form reality." Marcuse of course loathed the kind of thing represented by *Paradise Now* and the Greenwich Village experi-ment. "The gap which separates Art from reality," he writes, " . . . its 'illusory' character, can be reduced only to the degree to

25. Ibid., 24–25.

26. Stefan Brecht, "Revolution at the Brooklyn Academy of Music," *Tulane Drama Review* 13 (Spring 1969): 64; Bentley is cited in Patrick McDermott, "Portrait of an Actor, Watching," in the same journal, p. 78.

which *reality itself* tends toward Art as reality's own form." This can happen only in a qualitatively different society, one in which might be experienced what Marx called "the sensuous appropriation of the world." In the utopia depicted in William Morris's *News from Nowhere,* life has so thoroughly taken on the form of art that art as we know it—literary art in particular—has become superfluous. "Look!" says Ellen, laying her hands on the shoulders of the two lovers, "look! these are our books in these days!" It seems unlikely that this particular threat to art is imminent, but until the good life is truly upon us it would be well to protect the traditional rhetorical frame which has set art at a decent distance from reality.[27]

The persona is a device which helps perpetuate that distance. In doing so, says Mr. Davie, it prevents poets from breaking out of the nets of rhetoric, prevents them from speaking the truth about themselves. How to speak the truth about oneself?—it is an obsessive preoccupation of our time, almost as obsessive as its obverse, that question which is the signature of the twentieth century: Who am I? Jean-Paul Sartre talked of the problem in an interview a few years before his death. The only way Sartre can tell the truth about himself, he says, is in a fiction. *Les Mots,* his autobiography, is no truer than *La Nausée* or *Les Chemins de la Liberté.* "Not that the facts I report [in *Les Mots*] are not true, but *Les Mots* is a kind of novel also, a novel that I believe in, but that nevertheless remains a novel." In a better society, says Sartre, one could say the truth straight out: "I take up the pen, my name is Sartre, this is what I think." But that is impossible today: we do not know each other well enough; we cannot trust each other sufficiently. We must make do with fiction.[28]

It occurs to me that when Donald Davie calls for the abolition

27. Herbert Marcuse, *An Essay on Liberation* (Boston: Beacon Press, 1969), 24; "Art as a Form of Reality," in *On the Future of Art,* Intr. Edward F. Fry (New York: Viking, 1970), 131; William Morris, *News from Nowhere,* chap. 22. For discussion of the theme see Robert C. Elliott, "The Costs of Utopia," *Studies on Voltaire and the Eighteenth Century* 152 (1976): 677–92.

28. Michel Contat, "Sartre at Seventy: An Interview," trans. Paul Anster and Lydia Davis, *New York Review,* August 7, 1975, 12.

of the persona, for breaking down the barriers between literature and reality, he is really calling for a radically altered society, one in which it will be possible to say: "My name is Sartre, this is what I think." It is an ancient dream, an honorable one—the dream of utopia. I think we must continue to dream it, but only so long as we remember the propensity among searchers for utopia to end up in *Paradise Now*.

The Poet Never Lieth

Historians can hardly escape telling lies, says Sidney; but as for the poets, only a fool would accuse Aesop of lying in his stories about the beasts, and only a child would mistake a portion of a stage labeled Thebes for a city in Greece. The defense lasted for a long time. When Robert Herrick writes of amorous disasters:

> I have lost, and lately, these
> Many dainty Mistresses:
> Stately *Julia,* prime of all;
> *Sapho* next, a principall:
> Smooth *Anthea,* for a skin
> White, and Heaven-like Chrystalline:
> Sweet *Electra,* and the choice
> *Myrha,* for the Lute, and Voice.
> Next, *Corinna,* for her wit,
> and the graceful use of it:
> With *Perilla:* All are gone;
> Onely *Herrick's* left alone,
> For to number sorrow by
> Their departures hence, and die

readers would have identified "Herrick" within the poem with Robert Herrick the poet in a strictly limited sense only, and they certainly would not have worried about that Herrick's health. A poet in the Renaissance was not, as Wordsworth was to say, a man speaking to men, nor was his function to speak the truth about himself—the factual truth, that is; he was always concerned with a truth above the truth of fact. The poet was singer, performing within a representative role according to familiar and honored conventions. The question of truth to fact hardly arose. As Sidney said, "The poet never maketh circles about your imagination, to conjure you to believe for true what he writes."[29]

The situation changes radically in subsequent generations. As the values of the middle class become dominant, sincerity is widely endorsed as a standard to which poets are expected to conform, readers evince increasing interest in the persons and personalities of poets, and poets themselves turn inward, exploring their own beings and making poetry of the exploration. The speakers of their poems, who once enjoyed conventional life only, came to be more and more closely identified with actual authors, to the point where in some cases speaker and poet seem, and are intended to seem, identical. The ground of Sidney's defense has been abandoned as the poet deliberately conjures the reader "to believe for true what he writes."

> One evening...
> I went alone into a Shepherd's Boat,
> A Skiff that to a Willow tree was tied
> Within a rocky Cave, its usual home.
> .....; from the Shore
> I push'd, and struck the oars and struck again
> In cadence, ...
> It was an act of stealth
> And troubled pleasure. . . .
> She was an elfin Pinnace; lustily
> I dipp'd my oars into the silent Lake,
> And, as I rose upon the stroke, my Boat
> Went heaving through the water, like a Swan;
> When from behind the craggy Steep, till then the
>   bound of the horizon, a huge Cliff,
> As if with voluntary power instinct,
> Uprear'd its head. I struck, and struck again,
> And, growing still in stature, the huge Cliff

29. Sidney, *Apology for Poetry*, 123–24.

> Rose up between me and the stars, and still,
> With measur'd motion, like a living thing,
> Strode after me. With trembling hands I turn'd,
> And through the silent water stole my way
> Back to the Cavern of the Willow Tree.
> There, in her mooring-place, I left my Bark,
> And, through the meadows homeward went, with
>   grave
> And serious thoughts. . . .

The air of reality in this famous episode from *The Prelude* is unmistakable: who can doubt that the troubling theft took place in the world of history, that it was the real youth, William Wordsworth who committed it, or that it was a significant episode in the growth of a poet's mind? But then who, before reading Dorothy's *Journal,* could doubt the truth of that other episode of comparable significance in Wordsworth's life, in which Wordsworth himself seems to believe so strongly:

> He with a smile did then his words repeat;
> And said, that, gathering Leeches, far and wide
> He travelled; stirring thus about his feet
> The waters of the Ponds where they abide.
> "Once I could meet with them on every side;
> But they have dwindled long by slow decay;
> Yet still I persevere, and find them where I may."

The answer is of course that neither doubt nor belief of the kind implied is an appropriate response by a reader to any poetic statement. Thirty years ago Suzanne Langer taught us that poets deal in the language of their poems not with life, but with what she calls virtual life, which is as much an illusion as is the space created in a painting. Poetry, Langer says, is never a statement about historical fact; it creates a semblance, virtual history. "There is no trafficking with actualities in poetry, no matter how much the creator of the semblance has drawn on his own feelings, his deepest convictions, his memories and secret wishes. . . . [Poetry] does not express any proposition, and therefore does not advocate or confess anything.... Literary events are *made,* not reported, just as portraits are painted, not born and raised."[30]

The significance of Langer's work for literary criticism may have been partially obscured by the very range of her interests. *Feeling and Form* is a philosophical analysis of the modes of being of the major arts—music, painting and sculpture, the dance, as well as poetry, and there is an interesting appendix on the film. Some readers were doubtless put off by her specialized vocabulary: her use of the key term *virtual* was a problem. In any event, however, some of the problems Langer deals with have been engaged recently from a different perspective and with admirable lucidity and power of mind by Barbara Herrnstein Smith. Certain elements of Barbara Smith's work bear directly on the question of truth claims in literature and on the status of statements made by authorial "I's." They bear, that is, on the question of the persona.

Smith distinguishes between two kinds of discourse, natural discourse and fictive. By natural discourse she means all utterances that can be taken as the verbal acts of real persons on specific occasions in response to particular circumstances. A natural utterance is a historical event, occurring at a specific time and place, like any other event in the natural world. Poems (in the extended sense of the word) are not natural utterances; they *represent* such utterances; they are fictive. With poems the relationship between reader and author is entirely different from that obtaining between a listener and a speaker in natural discourse. The rules governing the former relationship are embodied in conventions, knowledge—and acceptance—of which enable us to distinguish the fictive from the natural situation. Drama provides the most obvious examples. There are many stories of untutored members of the audience at a play shouting warnings to the heroine, whose virtue is about to be attacked.

30. Suzanne K. Langer, *Feeling and Form* (London: Routledge, 1953), 211, 256–7, and throughout. Cf. George T. Wright in the first chapter of *The Poet in the Poem.*

Not really attacked, of course; the attack is *represented* as about to occur. The language and actions of the stage are mimetic or fictive discourse in the sense that they represent not actions or scenes or characters, but *discourse*. Poetry is not natural utterance but the representation of natural utterance. The point is not that the emotions expressed in a poem may be unreal, the events alluded to made up—the essential point is that the *"expressing and alluding are themselves fictive verbal acts."* Thus, says Smith, Keats's "Ode to Autumn" and Shakespeare's sonnets are precisely as fictive as "The Bishop Orders His Tomb" or Tennyson's "Ulysses."[31]

When in the first book of *The Prelude* Wordsworth writes

> One evening . . .
> I went into a Shepherd's Boat,

his statement sounds indistinguishable from what Barbara Smith calls a natural utterance; but because the statement occurs in a poem we accept the convention that it is not a statement saying something true (or false) about Wordsworth's experience in his youth, but is the *representation* of such a statement. Had Wordsworth uttered the identical words to Coleridge during a walk near Grasmere (perhaps he did utter them) they would have constituted a claim on truth. As it is, the "I" of "I went alone . . ." exists only in the poem, and the utterance affirms nothing about the world of history.[32]

Irvin Ehrenpreis's claim, "So long as there is no hint of deceitfulness, what a man says must be precisely what he means," expresses the fundamental principle upon which all *natural* discourse rests. Ehrenpreis, however, has in mind the statements of poets in their poems, and this is a very different matter indeed. Barbara Smith maintains that the suspension of the principle

31. Barbara Herrnstein Smith, *On the Margins of Discourse* (Chicago: University of Chicago Press, 1978), 15–50; "Poetry as Fiction," *New Literary History* 2 (1970–71): 268–71.

32. My friend David Antin has a poem in which he quotes a proposition of Ludwig Wittgenstein; the proposition has a different status with respect to truth inside the poem than it has outside, in natural discourse.

enunciated by Ehrenpreis is precisely what defines fictive discourse. There is no implication that the poet is lying: it is simply that he is not *saying,* in the usually accepted sense, at all. In another sense, of course, he is using fictive discourse to "say" something else, something meaningful, sincere, trivial, profound, whatever: the problem is to find the true subject. But the statements of poets in their poems are not part of natural discourse; they only *represent* natural discourse and hence are not subject to many of its claims.[33]

The same principle exactly applies to novels and tales, all efforts at realism notwithstanding. Writing from the point of view of speech-act theory, John Searle characterizes fictional utterances as "nonserious" (a spectacularly poor choice of terms), meaning that an author is not seriously committed to the claims made in his fiction as he would be if, seated in his study, he were to look out the window and say, "It is raining." A writer of fiction, says Searle, is engaged in a "nondeceptive pseudoperformance which constitutes pretending to recount to us a series of events." The fictional character of the text is identified by the illocutionary intentions of the author.

Novelists may use historical persons as characters, they may reproduce actual speech and documents and describe actual events; but if the materials were shaped by a novelist in the practice of his craft, the work in its entirety is fiction and makes no legitimate claim on historical truth. The fact that we can visit Napoleon's tomb but cannot find that of Prince Andrey, says Barbara Smith, does not make one part of Tolstoy's novel less fictional than another.[34]

33. Smith, *On the Margins,* 110–11.
34. John R. Searle, "The Logical Status of Fictional Discourse," in *Expression and Meaning* (Cambridge: Cambridge University Press, 1979), 60, 65. Smith, "Literature as Performance, Fiction, and Art," *Journal of Philosophy* 67 (1970): 560.

5 The Self and "t'other I"

It has been clear from the beginning of this investigation that the controversy over the persona has as an essential component sharply divergent beliefs about the nature of the self and personal identity. Attacks on the literary doctrine of the persona following on that of Bertrand Bronson, who, we recall, denounced the "schizoid notion of two Chaucers," have behind them a whole range of assumptions on these matters and their bearing on the interpretation of literature. Curiously, the notion of "two Chaucers" would probably not have disturbed a writer like Jonathan Swift who (his extraordinary literary experiments with the first person pronoun aside) casually comments on a fundamental "split" in his own personality. "But let me alone, sirrahs," he writes in the *Journal to Stella;* "for Pdfr is going to be very busy; not Pdfr, but t'other I." Here in the "little language" of the *Journal* Pdfr (pronounced Podefar and probably standing for Poor Dear Foolish Rogue) refers to Swift himself, one aspect of him, that is: the private Swift, relaxed in the intimacy of his relationship with his beloved Stella. "T'other I" is the public Swift, an impatient man, harassed by the turmoil of great affairs. Swift often splits himself this way in the *Journal,* playing the fool (a favorite role), then laughing at himself playing the fool. These

games generate interesting complexities in the *Journal:* "Answer
M D's [Stella's and Mrs. Dingley's] letter, Pdfr, d'ye hear? No,
says Pdfr, I won't yet, I'm busy: you're a saucy rogue. Who
talks?" A useful way to approach answering Swift's puzzling
question is to invoke the concept of the persona. It seems unlikely that Swift would have demurred.[1]

Taken at a different level, however, Swift's "Who talks?" is
almost equivalent to that terrible question, Who am I? which
for many years now, prompted by the modern passion for introspection, has produced epistemological nightmares. Swift
unquestionably recognized the problematic character of the self,
and his flirtations with chaos are famous; but his "not Pdfr,
but t'other I" implies no hint of the vertiginous depths which
our awareness of selves within selves has opened up.

Doubtless it is impossible to locate precisely the historical
point at which erosion of the idea of the unified, autonomous
self definitively set in. Jean Starobinski notes that Montaigne's
deliberate effort to step outside himself in order to observe himself initiates a process of infinite regress as observer observes
observer. According to Marxist theory the traumatic effects of a
developing capitalism may be seen in the altered image of the self
we find in the Renaissance. From another direction entirely the
sociologist Norbert Elias suggests that as in the history of Western man people learn to keep their bodily functions and sexual
activities private, they split their lives into public and private
spheres, developing modes of behavior and self-presentation
appropriate to each sphere. Thus a man or woman would present
one self in public, another in the unbuttoned privacy of lavatory
or bedroom—the domain, in some views, of the "real" self. Or,
another speculation: Georges Gusdorf follows Jacques Lacan in
specifying the invention at the end of the Middle Ages of the

1. Jonathan Swift, *Journal to Stella,* ed. Harold Williams, 2 vols. (Oxford:
Clarendon Press, 1948), 1:344; 2:380. (Williams follows Dean Swift in printing
Presto for Pdfr.) For good discussions of the rhetoric of the *Journal,* see Frederick
N. Smith, "Dramatic Elements in Swift's *Journal to Stella,*" *Eighteenth Century
Studies* 1 (1967–68): 332–52, and A. B. England, "Public and Private Rhetoric in
the *Journal to Stella,*" *Essays in Criticism* 22 (1972): 131–41.

silver-backed mirror as marking the historical moment when man crucially encountered his own image, with momentous psychological consequences. Robert Langbaum maintains that the self becomes problematic with Descartes and the English philosophers of empiricism. David Hume's denial of the idea of a determinate self, his disintegration of the concept of personal identity, is famous:

> It must be some one impression, that gives rise to every real idea. But self or person is not any one impression. . . . [We] are nothing but a bundle or collection of different perceptions, which succeed each other with an inconceivable rapidity, and are in a perpetual flux and movement. . . . The mind is a kind of theatre, where several perceptions successively make their appearance; pass, re-pass, glide away, and mingle in an infinite variety of postures and situations.

The idea of the self cannot be derived from any of these impressions, says Hume; consequently, "there is no such idea."[2]

Most sociologists interested in the concept of the self today accept something like Hume's conclusions, if not the precise terms of the model: to them the self, if there is such a thing, is basically unknowable. Their preferred approach to the problem is by way of role theory, which is rooted in ideas about primitive mentality advanced by Durkheim, Simmel, Lévy-Bruhl, and others. According to this view, any possibility of individual consciousness among primitive people is quite overwhelmed by the collective consciousness of the tribe. Consequently, a primitive man or woman has no sense of being a unique self, no

---

2. Jean Starobinski, "Montaigne on Illusion," *Daedalus,* Summer 1979, 93; Norbert Elias, *The Civilizing Process,* trans. Edmund Jephcott (New York: Urizen Books, 1978), 190; Georges Gusdorf, "Conditions and Limits of Autobiography," trans. James Olney in his *Autobiography: Essays Theoretical and Critical* (Princeton: Princeton University Press, 1980), 32–33; Robert Langbaum, *The Mysteries of Identity* (New York: Oxford University Press, 1977), 25ff; David Hume, *A Treatise of Human Nature,* ed. L. A. Selby-Bigge (Oxford: Clarendon Press, 1965), bk. 1, part 4, section 6, pp. 251–53. For a good present-day analysis of some philosophical problems associated with the concept of the self, see Henry W. Johnstone, Jr., *The Problem of the Self* (University Park, Pa.: Pennsylvania State University Press, 1970).

feeling of individuality: he cannot conceptualize ideas like self, person, or soul. Marcel Mauss argued in the Huxley Memorial Lecture of 1938, to which we referred in the second chapter of this book, that in primitive society individuals are established as persons *(personnages)* by virtue of the roles they play in the sacred dramas performed on ritual occasions. Those highly schematized roles, which are assigned on the basis of the individual's place in the kinship system, give a man his character; indeed, as with the kitchen maid in Proust, they *constitute* his character: "The kitchen-maid," writes Proust, "was an abstract personality, a permanent institution to which an invariable set of attributes assured a sort of fixity and continuity and identity throughout the long series of transitory human shapes in which that personality was incarnate; for we never found the same girl there two years running."[3]

Mauss claims, as we have seen, that the Romans, by giving the individual juridical status, transformed the notion of *personnalité mythique* into the notion of *personne morale* This latter is the familiar figure of contemporary sociology, the social person who today enacts a multiplicity of roles in his capacities as husband, father, lover, employee, employer, voter, team member, and so on, each role with its own ritual requirements. The roles, it is important to realize, are in this view wholly given by society: a person *is* the roles he plays, his expression of personhood ineluctably shaped by the social organization and culture into which he is born. Some such idea as this is basic to the work of ethnologists like Margaret Mead and sociologists like Erving Goffman. "I would maintain," writes Meyer Fortes in a passage cited earlier, "that the notion of the person in the Maussian sense is intrinsic to the very nature and structure of human society and human social behaviour everywhere." Clearly, such an idea of

3. See Fortes, "On the Concept of the Person among the Tallensi" (see chap. 2 n. 9 above), 283ff. I owe my knowledge of this important essay to Raymond D. Fogelson's "The Anthropology of the Self" (see chap. 2, n. 5 above). The Proust passage, cited by Fortes, is from *Swann's Way,* part 1, trans. C. K. Scott Moncrieff (London: Chatto and Windus, 1941), 106.

the self accommodates the concept of the persona with no difficulty whatever.[4]

Recent structuralist and poststructuralist theory in France goes even beyond the social scientists in abolishing traditional notions of the self. For Roland Barthes the "I" is no more than the wake of all the codes which are its sole constituent elements: subjectivity, as Barthes says in *S/Z,* is "not the ship but its wake, not the plow but its furrow." The linguistic "I," he says elsewhere, must be thought of in a completely a–psychological way. "I" is nothing other than (he quotes the linguist Emile Benveniste) "the person who utters the present instance of discourse containing the linguistic instance *I.*" Similarly, Lévi-Strauss, Lacan, Foucault, Derrida contribute in their various ways to the "decentering" of the subject. The self, personal identity, is at least as much an illusion to them as it was to David Hume.[5]

No matter how suspect the "I" may be in theory, however, in our lives and in the life of society we ignore theory and take as a given the existence of a more or less autonomous self. We may agree that the world outside us, including language, largely makes us what we are; but the theory that reduces us to the social systems or codes by which we are defined violates every person's sense that in him there is a residual area of freedom, of uniqueness, of I-ness.

William James's famous chapter ten of *The Principles of Psychology,* the chapter entitled "The Consciousness of Self," provides an influential model for those who cling to the belief that the self cannot be exhaustively defined by socially given roles and codes. Dividing the self into a hierarchy of categories—the material self, the social self, the spiritual self, pure ego—James recognizes that a person has as many social selves as there are

4. Fortes, 288.

5. Roland Barthes, "To Write: An Intransitive Verb?" in *The Structuralist Controversy,* ed. Richard Macksey and Eugenio Donato (Baltimore: Johns Hopkins University Press, 1970), 139. See Jonathan Culler, *Structuralist Poetics* (Ithaca: Cornell University Press, 1975).

distinct groups whose opinion he values. Those selves are markedly different from each other: "We do not show ourselves to our children as to our club-companions, to our customers as to the laborers we employ, to our own masters and employers as to our intimate friends." (The analogy here with the later concept of role playing is evident; and again it is clear that this concept easily accommodates the idea of the persona.) From this, says James, there results a splitting of the person into several selves, which may be discordant or harmonious, depending upon how the relations among the selves are managed.[6]

But unlike those social scientists today who find nothing beneath or beyond the roles one plays, James searches for a deeper self. A certain portion of the stream of consciousness (James's phrase) is felt to be an "innermost centre," a "sanctuary within the citadel" constituted by the circle of subjective life as a whole. Now, asks James, "what is this self of all the other selves," the self on which one would stake his salvation? James's answer is complex and beyond the scope of this inquiry; but that the central part of the self exists, he is in no doubt at all. We know that it exists, James says, because we *feel* it. "It is something with which we . . . have direct sensible acquaintance, and which is as fully present at any moment of consciousness in which it *is* present, as in a whole lifetime of such moments."[7]

As Erik Erikson points out, James's confidence in the existence of such a self did not prevent him from undergoing acute identity confusion in his dreams (James records the experience

6. William James, *The Principles of Psychology,* 2 vols. (London: Macmillan, 1907), 1:294.

7. James, 1:297ff. The notion that in moments of peril the mask is ripped off and the true self necessarily appears is very ancient. See Lucretius, *De Rerum Natura,* 3, lines 55–58: "quo magis in dubiis hominem spectare periclis convenit adversisque in rebus noscere qui sit; nam verae voces tum demum pectore ab imo eliciuntur ⟨et⟩ eripitur persona, manet res." "Wherefore it is more fitting to watch a man in doubt and danger, and to learn of what manner he is in adversity; for then at last a real cry is wrung from the bottom of his heart: the mask is torn off, and the truth remains behind." Trans. Cyril Bailey, in *Lucretius on the Nature of Things* (Oxford: Clarendon, 1921), 107–8. Cf. Montaigne, *Essays,* I, ix, "Of Liars."

of belonging simultaneously to three different dream systems, of being dreamed by a dream, like a character in Borges: *"Am I getting into other people's dreams?"* he asks); nevertheless, his introspective map has served as a model for those to whom the following brilliant evocation of selfhood by Gerard Manley Hopkins rings true in some basic way:

> ... my selfbeing, my consciousness and feeling of myself, that taste of myself, of *I* and *me* above and in all things, which is more distinctive than the taste of ale and alum, more distinctive than the smell of walnut leaf or camphor, and is incommunicable by any means to another man... this unspeakable stress of pitch, distinctiveness, and selving, this selfbeing of my own.[8]

That self, a version of James's self, is quite incompatible with the selves of the mechanistic models proposed by Freud, the behaviorists, and most (but not all) sociologists; they are mutually exclusive. Ralf Dahrendorf, a distinguished sociologist, points to the moral and philosophical dilemma sociology has made for itself by creating an artificial man, *homo sociologicus,* a depersonalized figure who is reduced in theory to the sum of his social roles, but whose experience disconfirms the theory countless times each day. The contradiction is radical; together with certain variations it constitutes a crucial element of the search for identity with which writers over the past two hundred years have been preoccupied. Wordsworth's *Prelude* is in an obvious sense a search for the self—a prime example of the creative mode Keats called the "egotistical sublime." It is less obvious that exploration of dramatic characters by the "camelion Poet"—Browning's of Andrea del Sarto, Tennyson's of Tithonus—are part of a similar quest; but Patricia Ball has argued persuasively that whether nineteenth-century poets write

8. Erik Erikson, *Identity: Youth and Crisis* (New York: Norton, 1968), 205ff; Gerard Manley Hopkins, "Comments on the Spiritual Exercises," in *Poems and Prose,* ed. W. H. Gardner (London: Penguin, 1953), 145–46—cited in Patricia Ball, *The Central Self* (London: Athlone Press, 1968), 224.

dramatically, as in the dramatic monologue, or write directly of themselves, they are fundamentally in search of their own identities. It is the urge to self-discovery that drives Robert Browning into taking on the personages of the characters he creates; it is his way of exploring human possibility and his own humanity.[9]

As every reader of contemporary literature knows, the search for the self continues unabated, although the spirit in which it is conducted has grown progressively darker. Many writers have gone past despair into comedy—black comedy like that of Beckett, or a cool, witty comedy like that of the poet Ed Dorn. "What's your name?" the Poet in Dorn's *Slinger* is asked. "I, I answered." Later, Lil, the madam of a Western whorehouse (an archetypal madam; she has been in the trade for two thousand years), observes that something is wrong with I.

> What happened to I she asked
> his eyes don't seem right.

The Poet reports:

> I is dead.

This remark might have come from a café in post-Sartrean Paris rather than from a coach in America's Wild West, and it has other associations with France as well. Whether deliberately or not, the grammatical disjunction links the Poet's statement in Dorn's poem with Rimbaud's "Je est un autre," the paradigmatic statement of the alienation from self which has become endemic in Western Culture. Transcending these dark implications, however, is a paradoxical circumstance, for the poet's act of recording the death of I contains an internal contradiction.

9. Ralf Dahrendorf, "Homo Sociologicus," in his *Essays in the Theory of Society* (Stanford: Stanford University Press, 1968), 25. For Keats's characterizations of the poet, see his letter to Richard Woodhouse, October 27, 1818, in *Letters,* ed. Hyder E. Rollins, 2 vols. (Cambridge: Cambridge University Press, 1958), 1:386–87. For Ball, see pp. 3, 213. Recent historical studies of the theme of identity as expressed in literature, both splendid, are Patricia M. Spacks, *Imagining a Self* (Cambridge, Mass.: Harvard University Press, 1976), and Robert Langbaum's *Mysteries of Identity.*

The existence of the poem in a major sense contravenes the death it has recorded. I is not dead as long as the poet speaks.[10]

The radical contradiction in our attitudes toward the self which Ralf Dahrendorf deplores unquestionably imposes a severe strain on our society, to say nothing of the strain on individuals. Other intellectual fields, however, have experienced comparable theoretical incompatibilities which, it has been shown, need not be finally debilitating. The most instructive example, coming from a very remote field, is that of physics. In the ensuing pages I shall follow closely Gerald Holton's essay on Niels Bohr, "The Roots of Complementarity," an essay, in my view, of potentially great value for humanistic study.[11]

Early twentieth-century physicists found themselves in a dilemma constituted by two radically different and incompatible descriptions of physical phenomena, the classical and the quantum descriptions. Einstein wrote in 1924: "We now have two theories of light, both indispensable, but, it must be admitted, without any logical connection between them, despite twenty years of colossal effort by theoretical physicists." All attempts to subsume the wave theory of light under the particle theory, or the particle theory under the wave theory, had failed. In 1927 Niels Bohr proposed that instead of trying to resolve the dichotomies physicists should recognize and accept their complementary nature. It was no longer possible, in his view, to reduce the wholeness of nature to a single, directly comprehensible model. The wholeness of nature was still there, despite the antithetical theories, but could be expressed only through a complementary mode of description.[12]

10. Edward Dorn, *Slinger* (Berkeley: Wingbow Press, 1975), bks 1 and 2.

11. Gerald Holton, "The Roots of Complementarity," in Holton, ed., *The Twentieth-Century Sciences: Studies in the Biographies of Ideas* (New York: W. W. Norton, 1972), 382–422. I. A. Richards frequently applied Bohr's ideas to literary problems; see his "Complementarities" in the collection of his essays under the same title edited by John Paul Russo (Manchester: Carcanet Press, 1976), 108–26.

12. The quotation from Einstein is in Holton, 384.

Bohr realized that however far the phenomena being studied may transcend, in his words, *"the scope of classical physical explanation, the account of all evidence must be expressed in classical terms."* This fact, as Bohr says, makes it impossible to impose a clear separation between the behavior of an atomic "object" and the experimental equipment used to study it. The system being observed and the instruments employed to make possible the observation form an inseparable whole, so that the choice of apparatus will determine the kind of results one gets. Thus with respect to light, any given experiment will show only one aspect of the matter: it is impossible to set up an experiment exhibiting simultaneously the wave properties of light and the particle properties. They are complementary.[13]

Niels Bohr's efforts to illustrate and make clear the principles of complementarity took him outside the field of physics and into areas of discussion which have direct and interesting bearing on our own enterprise. Colleagues and students who worked with Bohr recall the urgency with which he recommended what he called the "little book": *The Adventures of a Danish Student* by Poul Martin Møller, a nineteenth-century poet and philosopher. Everyone close to Bohr at the Institute for Theoretical Physics (in Copenhagen) became familiar with the book as part of his initiation into the ideas of complementarity. Bohr found in it material of direct consequence for his theory, in particular a passage in which a student tries to explain what it is that has kept him from getting a job:

> My endless enquiries make it impossible for me to achieve anything. Furthermore, I get to think about my own thoughts of the situation in which I find myself. I even think that I think of it, and divide myself into an infinite retrogressive sequence of "I"s who consider each other. I do not know at which "I" to stop as the actual, and in the moment I stop at one, there is indeed again an "I" which stops at it. I become confused and

13. Niels Bohr, "Discussion with Einstein on Epistemological Problems in Atomic Physics," in *Atomic Physics and Human Knowledge* (New York: John Wiley, 1958), 39–40. See Holton, 383–87.

feel a dizziness as if I were looking down into a bottomless abyss, and my ponderings result finally in a terrible headache.

As Holton shows, the passage represented for Bohr a situation analogous to that found in quantum physics. The student becomes dizzy because "thought" and "thinking about thought" are complementary with respect to each other. As he looks within himself the student obtrudes as an observer upon his own thought processes in the way that a macroscopic laboratory intrudes upon the submicroscopic events being studied. The analogy here in Bohr's view was not the usual amorphous analogy drawn between vaguely similar situations in remote fields; it was a "deep analogy," a clear example, in his words, of "logical relations which, in different contexts, are met with in wider fields."[14]

It seems likely that Bohr's interest in the problems of psychology and their relation to the field of atomic physics stems from his reading of William James. The first sentence of "The Stream of Thought," chapter nine of James's *Principles of Psychology,* is this: "We now begin our study of the mind from within"; and from that point on James encounters problems similar to those that baffled the physicists. Holton shows how remarkably similar the approaches of James and Bohr actually were. For example, James writes of consciousness that it flows: "Let us call it the stream of thought, or consciousness, or of subjective life." It is impossible, he says, introspectively to isolate parts of that stream for examination. If thoughts "are but flights to a conclusion, stopping them to look at them before the conclusion is reached is really annihilating them." Or if we are nimble enough to arrest a thought, "it ceases forthwith to be itself. . . . The attempt at introspective analysis in these cases," says James, "is in fact like seizing a spinning top to catch its motion, or trying to turn up the gas quickly enough to see how the darkness looks." In a similar way Møller's Danish student found it impossible to

14. Bohr quotes the passage from Møller in "The Unity of Human Knowledge," *Essays 1958–1962 on Atomic Physics and Human Knowledge* (New York: Interscience Publishers, 1963), 13. See Holton, 398–400.

allow his thoughts to flow freely while making them the subject of introspective analysis: as Holton says, these are mutually exclusive experimental situations.[15]

Bohr's high regard for the work of William James is well attested, and his enthusiastic use of Møller's little book as a heuristic device caused wide comment, and perhaps some puzzlement, among his colleagues and students in theoretical physics. But transference of an original mode of thought from one domain of knowledge to another is always difficult. Bohr was convinced that the principle of complementarity was applicable not only in physics but in psychology, anthropology, philosophy, biology, and a number of other areas as well. Indeed, he thought of it as the foundation of a new epistemology.

The story of the Danish student continued to intrigue him. Léon Rosenfeld, a close associate of Bohr for many years, writes of that interest:

> He could now look back at the duality of aspects of psychical experience with all the mastery he had acquired over the nature of complementarity relations, and point out that this duality corresponded to different ways of drawing a separation between the psychical process which was chosen as the object of observation and the observing subject: drawing such a separation is precisely what we mean when we speak of fixing our attention on a definite aspect of the process; according as we draw the line, we may experience an emotion as part of our subjective feeling, or analyze it as part of the observed process. The realization that these two situations are complementary solves the riddle of the [student's] egoes observing each other, and is in fact the only salvation from his qualms.[16]

---

15. James, *Principles of Psychology*, 1:239–44; Holton, 403–4. Bohr writes: "In introspection it is clearly impossible to distinguish sharply between the phenomena themselves and their conscious perception." To speak of directing attention to some aspect of psychical experience is to speak of mutually exclusive situations: between thought and feeling a complementary relationship exists. "Natural Philosophy and Human Cultures," *Atomic Physics and Knowledge*, 27.

16. Léon Rosenfeld, in Holton, 414.

It seems likely that the principle of complementarity can solve, or help to solve, many riddles beyond those of the Danish student. For example, the theories of Mauss, Goffman, Fortes, and others about the constitutive role of society in forming the self have great explanatory power—theories of this order are indispensable for understanding the self—but they lead to an artificial creation: Dahrendorf's "homo sociologicus," which violates our experience of our own being. The logically incompatible theories of those who follow William James's notion of a "self of all the other selves," the existence of which we know because we *feel* it, depend upon persuasive but essentially unverifiable criteria. These dichotomies may well be like the wave/particle theories of the physicists—dichotomies that instead of trying to reconcile we should accept as complementary to each other. Human beings exist as social as well as subjective persons; their wholeness can be expressed only through a complementary mode of description.

Jerome Bruner's account of a conversation he had with Niels Bohr illustrates beautifully the humanistic applicability of Bohr's theory:

> The talk turned entirely on the complementarity between... perception and reflection [Bohr] told me that he had become aware of the psychological depths of the concept of complementarity when one of his children had done something inexcusable for which he found himself incapable of appropriate punishment: "You cannot know somebody at the same time in the light of love and the light of justice!"[17]

17. Jerome Bruner, in Holton, 411. See Bohr's elaboration of this insight in "Unity of Knowledge," *Atomic Physics and Knowledge,* 81.

Part 3

Jonathan Swift

"Although Swift had some of the highest qualities necessary to the dramatist . . . the central dramatic faculty—that of detachment from his subject—was entirely wanting in him. . . . He is at once presenter and thing presented; nay more, operator and subject, a vivisector of himself, and of humanity through himself."

George Saintsbury, *The Peace of the Augustans: a Survey of Eighteenth Century Literature as a Place of Rest and Refreshment* (1916)

6 Swift's "I"

The lineaments of a new Jonathan Swift have been emerging in the last few years as critics reinterpret his work and find behind it an unfamiliar face. Instead of the arrogant Dean we know, slashing about with contempt and fury at a world he despised, a Swift is being discovered who repeatedly and from the beginning identifies himself with the victims of his own scourge. In *A Tale of a Tub,* it is said, "we are often hard-pressed to distinguish between Swift's voice and the voices of those he ridicules, because they all bespeak their mutual involvement in the ridiculous tragedy of the human predicament." Swift doesn't know whether to laugh or weep at the spectacle of his own and other men's folly; he is "stretched on the tough rack of his own satiric vision." Thus Gardner Stout in a recent essay. Irvin Ehrenpreis differentiates Swift from all those satirists who refuse to accept their own responsibility for the triumph of evil; unlike them, Swift "admits his own complicity" in the wickedness he attacks. By including his own case as an object of satire, Swift forces us, as readers, "to admit we helped perpetrate the crime we deplore." In short, the features of this newly discovered Swift seem closer to those of Baudelaire—"Hypocrite lecteur,—mon semblable,—mon frère!"—than to those of the man in whom Swift professed to have found his character, La Rochefoucauld.[1]

We have had romanticized Swifts before, but none, I think, so guilt-ridden, so willing to bare his guilt to the multitude—none so remote from Swift's avowal of his own motives: "Drown the World, I am not content with despising it, but I would anger it if I could with safety." The question of where this implausible Swift comes from is of considerable interest for the light it throws on the relation of interpretative procedures to interpretative results. To get down to it, I think that the picture of the new Swift comes from a mistaken way of dealing with issues arising when an author writes in the first person under an assumed character; it comes, in short from ignoring the idea of the persona.

The doctrine of the mask or persona has been particularly important in Swift studies, largely in reaction to easy identifications of author and character, as in Carl Van Doren's "Swift would have remained with the Houyhnhnms for ever if they had not sent him away." To dramatize the distinction between them it was found useful to cite the words of the *Travels* as Gulliver's words, thereby implying that Swift's meanings were likely to be very different from those of his persona. *A Tale of a Tub* had no handy name by which to identify its purported author, so labels were invented: the Hack, the Tale-teller, the Modern, etc. So with *A Modest Proposal* and its projector—the labels again serving to dramatize the distinction between the "I" of the mask in question and the true author. However, as this mode of criticism grew more popular, the dramatization tended to get out of hand: some interpreters imputed to Swift's personae the kind of substantial life normally associated with characters in George Eliot. Gulliver and even the Tale-teller were analyzed as though their

1. Gardner Stout, Jr., "Speaker and Satiric Vision in Swift's *Tale of a Tub*," *Eighteenth-Century Studies* 3 (1969): 196; Ehrenpreis, "Swift and the Comedy of Evil," in *The World of Jonathan Swift*, ed. Brian Vickers (Oxford: Blackwell, 1968), 217–18.

characters (such as they were) had intrinsic interest; the very word *persona* took on a magical aura.[2]

This reification of Swift's characters, and indeed the use of the persona at all, has called forth strong objections from distinguished scholars. It is nonsense, wrote Sir Herbert Davis, to interpose "this wretched 'Hack'" between Swift and the readers of *A Tale of a Tub*. Ehrenpreis insists that in *A Modest Proposal* there is no intermediate person between Swift and us as readers: the work makes sense only if we "treat the voice as the author's throughout."[3]

That phrase—it is the author's voice throughout—comes up again and again in the controversy over the persona. What an odd phrase it is, as one thinks of it. Clearly tautological—what other voice is there in a literary work?—its main thrust is toward method and has to do with how we should come to terms with the harlequin inconsistencies in Swift's personations. Of course on one level it is misleading to speak of voices at all: what we have are silent words on a printed page, but our metaphors retain the sense of persons speaking—dramatis personae—whose tones and inflections we "hear" through what Stephen Spender calls in a poem the "listening eye." We find it hard to speak of the actions of the printed page without recourse to terms from the pre-Gutenberg era.

In any event it is certain that our author's voice is heard throughout. The question is whether the voice should be heard as issuing directly from Swift's own mouth or through the mediation of spokesmen he has invented. Anti-persona critics propose that we should imagine Swift "performing" his works—*A Tale of a Tub,* for example—before friends. Gardner Stout puts the case well:

2. Carl Van Doren, *Swift* (New York: Viking, 1930), 195. Or again, "On his icy, fiery travels among the Houyhnhnms, Swift (why call him Gulliver?)...," 193.

3. Herbert Davis, review of Ronald Paulson, *Theme and Structure in Swift's Tale of a Tub,* in *Review of English Studies* n.s. 12 (1961): 301; Ehrenpreis, "Personae," in his *Literary Meaning and Augustan Values,* 59.

In telling his *Tale of a Tub,* Swift acts out the vices of the mob before the delighted eyes of his elite audience. The *Tale*'s rhetoric generally suggests an image of Swift, sitting with his fellow wits in an Augustan drawing-room and saying: a Wotton, a Bentley, a bookseller, a hack, a Rosicrucian *adeptus* talks thus—and then striking a pose and personating them, while simultaneously carrying on an ironic (often sarcastic) running commentary on their absurdities. Far from supposing that they are listening to an actual fool, this audience, Swift assumes, will recognize that they are listening to a master mimic and parodist.

The form of the drama set up in one's mind tends to affect the way one reads a given passage. Consider the following from *A Tale of a Tub:*

> I my self, the Author of these momentous Truths, am a Person, whose Imaginations are hard-mouth'd, and exceedingly disposed to run away with his *Reason,* which I have observed from long Experience, to be a very light Rider, and easily shook off; upon which Account, my Friends will never trust me alone, without a solemn Promise, to vent my Speculations . . . for the universal Benefit of Human kind.

If one thinks of Swift acting this out in the drawing-room, then one hears him delivering the passage in his characteristic wry, mocking tone, doubtless with a heavy accent on "momentous Truths"; but it seems reasonable to detect as well, as Stout and Ehrenpreis and others do, an obvious self-referential implication. Swift mocks the Bedlamite world he describes, but simultaneously, through his use of the first person, admits complicity in it. So it is claimed.[4]

On the other hand, the persona critic considers that the passage just quoted is uttered by a character whom Swift has

---

4. Stout, "Speaker and Satiric Vision," 183. All quotations from *A Tale of a Tub* are from the edition by A. C. Guthkelch and D. Nichol Smith, 2d ed. (Oxford: Clarendon Press, 1958); the quoted passage is from "A Digression on Madness," 180. For an excellent discussion of these issues see the recent article by Frederic V. Bogel, "Irony, Inference, and Critical Uncertainty," *Yale Review* 69 (Summer 1980): 503–19.

created, an egregious Modern, no more (and no less) to be identified with Swift than, say, Folly is with Erasmus. To be sure, the character who tells the *Tale* shares with his creator a dazzling play of fancy and an incredible virtuosity in language: Shakespeare's voice is heard in Dogberry as well as Hamlet, and this is still Jonathan Swift speaking through the mask. This internal contradiction arises whenever a linguistically gifted writer personates a foolish or illiterate spokesman. Stephen Gilman comments on *Lazarillo de Tormes:* "How quickly we overcome our surprise that a person born and brought up as Lazarillo was born and brought up should become one of the most effective writers of Castilian ever to practice the art!" In fact, we accept the contradiction as part of our surrender to the fictive premises of the work.[5]

Swift manipulates matters, however, so that his narrator opts for the false values and idiotic positions characteristic of all that Swift despises. He is by no means a consistent figure as in his representative character he modulates laterally from one species of folly to another (each identifiable in contemporary culture and, as later with Pope's Dullness, each tending to the same evil end) and vertically from sheer imbecility through erratic brilliance to "accidental" insights worthy of Swift. At regular intervals, however, as though in self-protection, as a means of maintaining ironic control over his explosive material, Swift sees to it that his spokesman anchors himself firmly, as "a most devoted Servant of all *Modern* Forms," in all that Swift is not. In my view this way of envisaging matters makes it more difficult to slide into the facile identifications which make Swift a principal target of his own satire. He may be a target—I think he is—but at a level different from the one proposed.

If it is true that Swift's voice is heard throughout, it is equally true that he has, as we say, many voices:

> O thou! Whatever Title please thine ear
> Dean, Drapier, Bickerstaff, or Gulliver!

5. Stephen Gilman, "The Death of Lazarillo de Tormes," *PMLA,* June 1966, 152.

—to say nothing of projectors, Examiners, madmen, and the like. In all the cacophony issuing from the throats of these spokesmen the task of the interpreter is always to try to distinguish the true voice, the one that speaks authentically for the author. The task is immensely difficult. In one sense every character in a created work speaks for the author; that is, each is an agency through whom the author speaks—hence the appropriateness of the term *persona* with its notion of mask through which the actor and, by way of him, the dramatist communicate with us. Then, as many writers have said, the author not only speaks through but in some sense *is* each of his characters, all of whom have lived powerfully in his imagination; their thoughts, their acts have been his. "Everything derives from the author," writes André Gide. "All the heaven and hell of his characters is in him." It is something of this kind that Coleridge meant when he said that Shakespeare becomes all things, yet forever remains himself. In Gide's sense, then, Shakespeare "is" Hamlet, but also Iago and Malvolio; just as Flaubert "is" Madame Bovary; just as Swift (although he created no characters comparable to these) "is" what he incorporated in the persons of Gulliver or the Tale-teller or any other of his fictional spokesmen or impersonations.

Clearly, however, the "is" in this identification contains a cloud of ambiguities and endless possibilities of reductive assimilations. Authors, confronted by such reductions, have naturally enough expressed their restiveness. "I had not been Jack Burden," writes Robert Penn Warren, "except insofar as you have to try to 'be' whatever you are trying to create. And in that sense, I was also Adam Stanton, and Willie Stark, and Sadie Burke, and Sugar Boy, and all the rest." Thus in certain carefully defined respects the identification of "I" and author holds, but in others it is ridiculous. At the deepest level of his personality—below the level of consciousness, of ego, of moral judgment: at the source of creativity—Shakespeare can be said to have been, or to have contained within himself, all that Iago was: in his imagination Shakespeare committed Iago's deeds and I daresay paid whatever psychological price is exacted for trafficking in such evil. Even at the conscious level it seems probable that Shakespeare recognized the potentiality of an Iago in himself. But between potentiality and act lies everything that makes the critical human difference: few moral systems any longer maintain that to have imagined an evil is to have committed it. When Kenneth Burke writes of Thomas Mann's "sympathy with the abyss" and claims that within Mann's work are all the errors of the Nazis, he is careful to add the crucial corollary: Mann encompasses these errors within a wider frame, giving them a totally different ontological and moral status to that they would have had in their "pure" form outside the literary work. Dostoevski may in some obscure sense "be" Raskolnikov, and unquestionably in his imagination he committed Raskolnikov's crime, but in any sane moral system he cannot be said to bear Raskolnikov's guilt.[6]

The most interesting issue in Swift studies today is the question of Swift's guilt and his willingness to express consciousness of it in his satire. Ehrenpreis distinguishes Swift from writers like Juvenal, Molière, Brecht on the grounds that the latter do not bring themselves as targets into their own works and accept no responsibility for the evils they depict. In contrast, he holds, Swift's method of identifying himself with the object of attack makes him a participant in the evil in question and so a target of his own satire. Ehrenpreis cites as an example the *Letter of Thanks from My Lord Wharton* (1712) in which Swift writes in the person of the infamous Wharton. By taking on that identity, says Ehrenpreis, Swift "plunges into the prospect of evil, establishing himself in the immediate foreground of the scene." I find this a very strange notion. According to it, when Swift writes in the earlier *A Short Character of Lord Wharton* (1710), "He [Wharton] is a Presbyterian in Politics, and an Atheist in Religion; but he

6. Robert Penn Warren, Introduction to the 1974 English edition of *All the King's Men* (London: Secker and Warburg), xiv; Kenneth Burke, *Philosophy of Literary Form* (Baton Rouge, La.: Louisiana State University Press, 1941), 48–49. Stendhal, a great impersonator himself, claims that Byron despised Shakespeare "for having been able to transform himself into Shylock, a vile Venetian Jew, or Jack Cade, a contemptible demagogue." "Lord Byron in Italy," in *Selected Journalism,* ed. Geoffrey Strickland (London: John Calder, 1959), 306.

chuseth at present to whore with a Papist," Swift (like Molière and Brecht) stands aloof from the object of attack and apparently is himself unscathed by it; but when in the *Letter of Thanks* he writes (in the person of Wharton), "This you say is the Opinion of Christ, St. *Peter,* and St. *Paul:* And 'faith I am glad to hear it; for I never thought the Prigs had been Whigs before," the act of writing "I" places Swift himself in the moral context of Wharton, thus making him the object of his own satire. Ehrenpreis uses this bit of moral one-upmanship as a criterion to distinguish Swift from Pope, who never, he says, dares admit his complicity in the sins he attacks. Pope always excludes his own case from the satire:

> Yes, I am proud; I must be proud to see
> Men not afraid of God, afraid of me.

"Swift," says Ehrenpreis, "by risking more, wins more."[7]

Doubtless there was risk even beyond that of dignity. Stories of what happens to men who enact the role of Judas in the passion play give a lurid point to the deep-rooted belief that incautious personations can destroy the integrity of one's personality. It was surely an act of psychological daring for Swift to think himself into the mind of the loathed Wharton so that he could speak in his name. John Traugott writes of the gains attendant on that risk: "The fact is that we should not have Swift at all, his terrible truths...if his imagination did not work through the psychologies of the outrageous figures he officially hates. Their indecorums, their far-fetched metaphors, their absolute egotism fill his imagination, defrock the priest, and give us a radical and libertine thinker." We may compare Thackeray's comment to a friend about the composition of *The Newcomes:* "Mr. Pendennis is the author of the book, and he has taken a great weight off my mind, for under that mask and acting, as it were, I can afford to say and think many things that I couldn't venture on in my own person."[8]

7. Ehrenpreis, "Swift and the Comedy of Evil," 213–19.
8. On the dangers of impersonation, see Rousseau's *Lettre à M. d'Alembert;*

Swift takes on the guise of the enemy in order to do a wreck-
ing job from the inside; he wants to articulate and lay bare the
premises, to trace out the consequences, of the enemy's position.
His brilliant counterfeiting is dangerously convincing: the Lu-
cretian and Hobbesian roles fit as though they were his own. To
what degree Swift's method indicates a secret "sympathy with
the enemy"—and how secret that sympathy was from Swift
himself—one cannot know; but the fact is certain: when Swift
fantasizes himself into the skin of one he hates, extraordinary
energies are liberated. His irony was doubtless his way of de-
fanging the impermissible ideas that tormented him. By encom-
passing those ideas within the frame of his satiric fantasy he
makes legitimate his traffic with them, but the personal cost of
the entanglement must have been great.

But to impersonate the enemy, and even at some level of one's
being to have sympathy with him, is not, as critics are saying
now, automatically to take on the enemy's guilt or to admit
complicity in his acts. When the Tale-teller writes of his hard-
mouthed imagination's running off with his reason, I think it
mistaken to assert that at any conscious level Swift was thinking
of himself and expecting readers to think of the author behind
the mask. In the Digression on Madness the Tale-teller also
claims that he once had the happiness to be an unworthy
member of Bedlam. Are we to conclude that Swift had once
been locked up? How does one decide that the one statement is
self-referential, the other not? Clearly such a decision is made,
for the first passage has been cited by several writers as evidence
of Swift's admitting his complicity in the world's madness. The
second is never cited. And no one is tempted to identify Swift
with the L'Estranges and William Wottons whom he personates:
their folly has not the attractiveness that madness holds for our

---

Jane Austen's *Mansfield Park;* and Lionel Trilling, *"Mansfield Park,"* in *The Op-
posing Self* (London: Secker and Warburg, 1955), 206–30. A grisly instance: on
my own campus a brilliant student, scheduled to play Orestes in a local dramatic
performance, was charged with stabbing his mother to death with an antique
sword. The Thackeray quotation is from *Letters and Private Papers,* 4 vols., ed.
Gordon N. Ray (London: Oxford University Press, 1946), 4:436.

age. Thus, although impersonating the enemy must have had major psychological significance for Swift, I cannot see that the act itself has any peculiar moral or metaphysical virtue. The "I" of the *Letter of Thanks from My Lord Wharton* brings Jonathan Swift no more into the foreground of the prospect of evil than Tartuffe brings Molière or Arturo Ui brings Brecht; nor do the psychological risks entailed in writing "I" in the person of Lord Wharton confer literary merit.

The problem turns on the relation of the first person speaker in a literary work to the author, and of both to the reader—a relation perilous enough at best but immensely complicated by authorial irony. Ordinarily, when a writer commits his opinions and ideas to the printed page, the situation between him and his readers is like that of a man beginning a new social relationship. According to Erving Goffman, society is organized in such a way that upon entering the presence of others an individual "projects a definition of the situation and thereby makes an implicit or explicit claim to be a person of a particular kind." By this claim "he automatically exerts a moral demand upon the others, obliging them to value and treat him in the manner that persons of his kind have a right to expect." Conversely, he foregoes all claims to treatment that would be appropriate for someone other than he appears to be. In the literary situation, the author introduces himself to an unknown audience either in his own person or through a narrator (this is much oversimplified); the audience accepts the terms of the introduction, knowing that the "definition of the situation" is make-believe, but willingly suspending its disbelief. It expects that the terms announced at the beginning of the relationship will be maintained, that the words it reads are a true reflection of the character of the spokesman. These are the ground rules. Any major violation of the terms introduces into the relationship a severe perturbation.[9]

The notorious instability of Swift's personae in their relation to the author makes the relation author-spokesman-reader often painfully confused, the definition of the situation ambiguous.

9. Erving Goffman, *The Presentation of Self in Everyday Life* (London: Allen Lane, The Penguin Press, 1969; orig. pub. 1959), 1–14.

When Swift's spokesman in *A Tale of a Tub* identifies himself as "a most devoted Servant of all *Modern* Forms," or in *A Modest Proposal* says, "I recommend dressing them hot from the Knife," the extent of the ironic gap between the "I" who speaks and Swift himself is clear. When, however, his spokesman writes, "Satyr being levelled at all, is never resented for an offense by any," or "if it were not for the Assistance of Artificial *Mediums,* false Lights, refracted Angles, Varnish, and Tinsel; there would be a mighty Level in the Felicity and Enjoyments of Mortal Men," or in *A Modest Proposal,* "*perhaps I could name a Country, which would be glad to eat up our whole Nation without* [*salt*]," it is practically impossible to distinguish between the spokesman's voice and that of Swift. (We recognize Swift's voice because we have heard him uttering these or similar sentiments in more reliable contexts; they are well within the appropriate "horizon" invoked for Swift's work.) The persona moves back and forth on a scale ranging form antithesis to Swift to identification, the shifts usually being signaled by variations in tone. The identifications are rare, however; most of the time the persona is resolutely allied with the enemy.

Formal control over the irony occasionally lapses ("no man," says Jeremy Taylor in a sermon, "can long put on a person and act a part, but his evil manners will peep through the corners of the white robe"). As Carnochan notices, at one harrowing point in the *Modest Proposal* the projector reveals that for years he has worn himself out offering "vain, idle visionary Thoughts" to save Ireland—the same thoughts that Swift as a public man had himself proposed. The formal distance between mad projector and author all but collapses as the "I" who speaks is tied into the reality of Swift's life. Whether one thinks of the projector as a persona of Swift, or with Ehrenpreis and others reads the *Proposal* as issuing from Swift's voice throughout, the collision of two levels of reality—fantasy and fact—produces a moment of frightful illumination. This impersonation trespasses on the demonic; the risks involved in it are beyond calculating.[10]

10. W. B. Carnochan, *Lemuel Gulliver's Mirror for Man* (Berkeley: University of California Press, 1968), 114.

Normally in Swift's work, where ironic distance is carefully maintained, it is a very tricky business indeed to read from the "I" of the satire to the character of the man who created it. Psychoanalysts may make that leap following the rules of their mystery and obtaining results appropriate to their methods, but literary interpreters make it at grave peril. Even when Swift speaks out apparently *in propria persona,* thrusting aside his fictive spokesman (or, if one prefers, dropping the ironic pose), one can never be sure he is truly speaking—or speaking truly—for himself. The famous "Fool among Knaves" passage in section nine of *A Tale of a Tub,* one of the most baffling cruxes in Swift's work—it will be discussed in the next chapter—is a case in point. Or again, in *A Short View of the State of Ireland* (1728) Swift's spokesman utters a panegyric on the state of the country:

> the thriving numerous plantations, the noble Woods... the Towns and Villages, where every Body is busy, and thriving with all Kind of Manufactures... the comfortable Diet and Dress, and Dwellings of the People.

Suddenly comes an abrupt break in tone: "But my Heart is too heavy to continue this Irony longer," followed by a savagely despairing litany of Ireland's woes. The effect is dramatic: again two orders of reality collide, or seem to. It is like those strange moments in a Pirandello play when an actor steps out of character to remind the audience that he is a real person pretending to be somebody else. Then one realizes that in claiming to be speaking in his own voice about the real person he is, the actor may be impersonating "himself" just as completely as he was impersonating Pirandello's character. So Swift may be pretending to inject his true self into the essay as a rhetorical move: his heart may not have been too heavy to continue the irony, but he may have seen rhetorical advantage in claiming that it was (it gets him out of the panegyric mode, which was entered upon late in the essay and without motivation; it is a powerful guarantor of his sincerity, etc.). However unlikely one may find this interpretation, it is a defensible one and proof is unavailable in either case. "Whilst I am talking...in this easy chatty way," says Thackeray's narrator in *The Virginians,* "what right have you, my good sir, to know what is really passing in my mind? It may be that I am racked with gout." No one knew the advantages—the necessity—of artifice better than Swift, in whom, as Denis Donoghue says, "the relation between directness and obliquity is peculiarly delicate."[11]

The most extreme reaction against the use of the persona in Swift criticism is that of Donoghue, who is not, however, like Ehrenpreis, Stout, and others, concerned to bring the author back into the work. Quite the contrary. Donoghue recommends that we approach Swift's work as though it came from out of the void, as though its words issued from a printing press. It is at once fascinating and disturbing to encounter such an intelligent, wide-ranging book as Donoghue's conducted on interpretative principles at such variance with one's own. Writing under the influence of French structuralists, with their denigration of the subject, and of North American writers like Marshall McLuhan and Hugh Kenner, Donoghue believes that far too much attention has been directed to the characters who are the ostensible spokesmen of Swift's satires: the Tale-teller, Gulliver, the Irish projector, and the rest. "The book is an object," he writes, "ostensibly independent of its author: there is a corresponding sense in which the marks on the page may be cut adrift from their ostensible speaker. In an oral culture, this monster of dissociation would be impossible: in a visual or print culture, it is a constant resonance." Swift, Donoghue insists, is not Flaubert or James; his spokesmen are so shallowly conceived, so inconsistent and amorphous that their words should properly be severed from their persons, who are beside the point. To personalize in the slightest degree the speaker of, say, *A Tale of a Tub,* is a mistake. "We are reading words on a page; implying rather things being said than a voice saying them." The language

---

11. Denis Donoghue, *Jonathan Swift: a Critical Introduction* (Cambridge: Cambridge University Press, 1969), viii.

should be thought of as sourceless. "These words are bullets: the important consideration is their end, not their origin." It is an unfortunate image and turns back on its maker. To understand the meaning of any act—certainly any shooting—one must know the circumstances surrounding the act. In the recent history of both Ireland and the United States we can understand the significance of many killings only when we know where the bullets came from. Without that knowledge we can identify the victims and mourn as appropriate, but we cannot know the meaning of the event. So with satire. Swift delivers his bullets by way of the most unlikely agencies and in defiance of all laws of ballistics. If we want to know how his victims were done in, we are obliged to trace the projectiles backwards, like Hercules' oxen, to their source. Praise of his own dear native country in the mouth of Gulliver may convey a devastating criticism of England; similar praise from the Brobdingnagian king may constitute a standard of excellence of which Swift approves. The source is crucial. Even with the more amorphous "I" of *A Tale of a Tub* a certain minimal baseline of consistency in the persona's point of view is necessary (as we shall see in the next chapter) if the satire is not to disintegrate into chaos.[12]

All this pother about persona, voices, and the rest—however clumsily we put it—is only an effort to clarify ways to get at meaning. Ehrenpreis is perfectly right: we can forget about the persona and "deal directly with the satirist"—Swift's persona or Swift personating, it makes little difference—as long as the ground rules are clear. As it happens, however, it is extraordinarily difficult to stay within the governing conventions. If one drops the persona and wants to talk analytically about *A Modest Proposal,* one is likely to fall into the trap of saying "Swift recommends dressing them hot from the Knife." Donoghue, I think, gets caught from time to time. Refusing, programmatically, to locate any dramatic authority in Swift's personae, he sometimes ends up attributing to Swift zany sentiments

---

12. Donoghue, chap. 1. Donoghue has subsequently become a formidable antagonist of the deconstructive mode of criticism.

and attitudes expressed by those marks on the page which have been cut loose from the ostensible speaker. For example, he makes a good deal of Swift's delight in rhetorical reduction, then asserts that it is Swift—not the Tale-teller—who reduces *spiritus, animus, afflatus, anima* all to one word: *Wind.* It is Swift who insists that, far from being a microcosm, man is no more than a suit of clothes. And, climactically, in *The Mechanical Operation of the Spirit,* Donoghue says, Swift is trapped by his own reduction: the work is "the art of sinking in religion; its aim to speed the sinking." This criticism, focusing on intention, constitutes some of the harshest criticism of Swift since Thackeray. It ignores, in my view, the fact that Swift's rhetorical reductions are the agent in a multileveled and very funny satirical attack on, among other things, religious enthusiasm, scholastic doctrine, obscurantist philosophy, system building, and, above all, on reductivism itself. That Swift is taking terrible risks is unquestionable. But by ignoring the distinction between persona and author, Donoghue saddles Swift with the very idiocy he is attacking. It is an occupational hazard for a satirist, the power of whose language may be uncontainable.[13]

The temptation to slip into easy identification of "I" and author is increased substantially when for one reason or another the persona is ignored. Something of the kind must have happened to Ehrenpreis when he writes, of the Wharton impersonation, that Swift "plunges into the prospect of evil, establishing himself in the immediate foreground of the scene." Swift plunges all right, but he establishes Wharton, not himself, in the foreground. Again, writing of *The Mechanical Operation of the Spirit* Ehrenpreis speaks of Swift's consciousness of a dilemma: how as one of the damned himself can he recognize the general condi-

13. Donoghue, 45; cf. 94–95. Flamboyant sentiments of Shakespeare's characters are commonly attributed to the playwright. A front-page story in the *Los Angeles Times* (August 30, 1976) on a proposal to relieve congestion in the law courts carried this epigraph: "'The first thing we do, let's kill all the lawyers.' Shakespeare, King Henry VI (1591)." A *New York Times* writer (financial section, January 6, 1980) says that Shakespeare dismisses gold as "the common whore of mankind."

tion? "Normally," says Ehrenpreis, "Swift's resolution is ironical. By classifying himself among the accused, he forestalls the accusations of others." The classification is apparently effected by the simple act of writing "I" and putting damning words in the "I"'s mouth. At some deep level of the psyche we may guess that the identification holds. It may even hold more firmly than if Swift had written "he." I think William Empson was justified in speaking of the "fearful case of Swift" who pretended "too convincingly" to believe that "all religion is really a perversion of sexuality," just as William Blake was justified in saying that Milton was of the devil's party without knowing it. But as Ehrenpreis maintains, "The province of literary meaning belongs to the public domain." That Swift consciously associated himself with the nihilistic storm generated by the ideas he developed in parody, I think wholly unlikely; and that as a matter of literary strategy he associated himself with the accused, I think incredible. "We cannot," writes Claude Rawson, "imagine him ever saying, 'Lemuel Gulliver, c'est moi.'" The concept of the persona, requiring a distinction between poetic and the empirical "I," will not guarantee correct reading of vexed passages in Swift and similar writers, but it does offer stout resistance to fatally easy identifications.[14]

Ehrenpreis's objections to the persona theory have been convincingly answered, in my view, by Maynard Mack's *The Garden and the City,* a book that shows in the most concrete and particular way how, at Twickenham, Alexander Pope "evolved over the years a setting that expressed him and at the same time helped nourish in his consciousness the dramatic personality who speaks to us from the satires and epistles of the 1730s—a personality who is at once the historical Alexander Pope and the fictive hero of a highly traditional confrontation between virtuous simplicity and sophisticated corruption." Mack does not use

14. Irvin Ehrenpreis, *Swift: the Man, His Works, and the Age* (London: Methuen, 1962), 1:246; William Empson, *Some Versions of Pastoral* (London: Chatto and Windus, 1950), 60; C. J. Rawson, "Cannibalism and Fiction," I, *Genre* 10 (Winter 1977): 684.

the term *persona* in connection with this figure whose creation he recapitulates so beautifully, perhaps because of the battering the word has taken since his essay "The Muse of Satire" of thirty years ago; but it is clear that the whole book is in effect a demonstrative proof of the thesis of that essay.[15]

A final reason for retaining the persona is that he is there at the author's insistence:

> Having long considered the gross Abuse of Astrology in this Kingdom; upon debating the Matter with my self, I could not possibly lay the Fault upon the Art, but upon those gross Impostors, who set up to be the Artists. I know, several learned Men have contended, that the whole is a Cheat; that it is absurd and ridiculous to imagine, the Stars can have any influence at all upon human Actions, Thoughts, or Inclinations: And whoever hath not bent his Studies that Way, may be excused for thinking so, when he sees in how wretched a Manner this noble Art is treated, by a few mean illiterate Traders between us and the Stars; who import a yearly Stock of Nonsense, Lies, Folly, and Impertinence, which they offer to the World as genuine from the Planets; although they descend from no greater a Height than their own Brains.

This is not sourceless language. By his style in this opening address to the public, Isaac Bickerstaff defines himself, he sets the terms that will govern the contractual relationship of his readers with him and with his creator. His "projection of the situation" is one we accept; and although we may be occasionally tricked as the terms are temporarily violated, this is the contract that governs the entire work.[16]

15. Maynard Mack, *The Garden and the City* (Toronto: University of Toronto Press, 1969), 8.

16. Jonathan Swift, "Predictions for the Year 1708," in *Prose Works,* ed. Herbert Davis (Oxford: Blackwell, 1939), 2:141.

7

Swift's Satire

Rules of the Game

Claude Rawson says in his splendid essay "Order and Cruelty" that the discussion of character in Swift's satires leads to deserts of circularity. This is true if we approach character in the usual novelistic sense, explaining specific utterances by reference to personality or cultural traits of the speaker, matching word and deed to motive within a frame of psychological consistency, and so on. On the other hand, to dismiss the question of character in Swift's works—to go along with Denis Donoghue, for example, who, as we have seen, recommends that we think of the language of *A Tale of a Tub* as sourceless, ignoring the character of the speaker entirely—won't do, if only because that would be to dismiss the fundamental fictive postulate on which the satirist bases his work. When in any work of the imagination the author creates a spokesman, tells the reader (as Swift does in the *Tale*) who the spokesman is, why he is writing, what his qualifications are, something of the kind of person he is (no matter in how mocking a way), all this has both purpose and function. A major function of Swift's impersonations—as a mad Modern, an Irish projector, as Gulliver—is that they allowed him to think himself into the heart of evil, to traffic with the impermissible; and if we are ever to understand the results of those encounters, it will have to be by way of the creatures under whose protection he ventured.[1]

Swift's feats of impersonation operate according to rules which every reader senses but which no critic I know of has been able to specify very precisely. The game is this: Swift must express himself through a zany alter ego, say truth by means of a lie, speak sense through a madman's lips. He must manipulate a persona whose utterance simultaneously expresses and unwittingly condemns the folly Swift is pursuing. As for the reader, his part in the game is to follow the complex maneuvers as closely as possible, recreating them in his own mind as he is flung wildly about, from rides on broomsticks and flying islands to plunges into Bedlamite horrors. Curiosity—that "Spur in the Side, that Bridle in the Mouth, that Ring in the Nose of a lazy, impatient, and a grunting Reader"—keeps him going through *A Tale of a Tub*: curiosity to konw where the ideas lead, of course, but in an important sense, curiosity to know whether Swift in the crazy guise he has assumed can keep his footing in the perilously intricate dance he has set in motion. To keep footing means to follow the rules of the game.

The most important rules governing *A Tale of a Tub* as well as the other satires have to do with the functioning of Swift's fictional spokesmen, with (in some sense) character, for although these spokesmen are not refugees from the novel or from drama and cannot be expected to follow the conventions of those very different games, there are unmistakable "family resemblances" between them and the personages of better-understood literary forms. Perhaps these can best be seen from a negative perspective. In the novel a writer's initial commitment to a tone, a style, a mode of being for his spokesman limits drastically the possibilities for development in the ensuing work. After the opening pages of their respective novels Fielding could not have married Sophia to Blifil, Jane Austen could not have

1. C. J. Rawson, "Order and Cruelty," *Essays in Criticism* 20 (1970): 24–56; reprinted in *Gulliver and the Gentle Reader* (London: Routledge and Kegan Paul, 1973), 33–59; Donoghue, *Swift,* 5–9.

allowed Elizabeth Bennet to catch a fever and die. As the information theorists say, the early paragraphs of these novels contain a significant element of redundancy, as do most literary works. Think of the immense ranges of experience the first lines of *Paradise Lost* rule out for Milton.

The principle operates in a similar (although less exclusive) way even in a maverick work like *A Tale of a Tub*. As we have it now, the *Tale* opens with an Apology, which is extrinsic to the *Tale* proper, and with some pleasant mystifications from the bookseller; the first words spoken by the Tale-teller who is the source of all that follows are these in the Dedication to Prince Posterity:

> *Sir,*
> I here present *Your Highness* with the Fruits of a very few leisure Hours, stollen from the short Intervals of a World of Business, and of an Employment quite alien from such Amusements as this: The poor Production of that Refuse of Time which has lain heavy upon my Hands, during a long Prorogation of Parliament, a great Dearth of Forein News, and a tedious Fit of rainy Weather.

The self-characterization in this utterance is enough to trigger an elaborate scanning process on the part of the reader—a process that, negatively, allows him to rule out many possibilities in the way the *Tale* might develop; one that, positively, gives him clues enabling him to guess at what kind of game he is entering on. From our initial impression of any work we intuit a sense of the whole, without which, as E. D. Hirsch says, any individual trait of the work would be rootless and without meaning. As we read further, of course, we refine our sense of the whole accommodating new details, adjusting our expectations, ruling out what had once seemed possibilities until, firmly involved in the hermeneutic circle, we approximate a grasp of the appropriate rules. But from the beginning our sense of the whole is grounded in our reading of the source of all our information: in *A Tale of a Tub* it is the crack-brained Modern whose genius lies, as he tells us, in devising tubs for the amusement of leviathanic wits.[2]

Doubtless "character" is an inadequate word here: we are not speaking of a coherent personality or intellectual position. Rawson, who has a splendid way with language, speaks of the Tale-teller as "an amorphous mass of disreputable energies." Nevertheless, because those energies are associated with a designated speaker, certain renunciations that we normally associate with "character" as understood in other genres necessarily are involved. For example, amorphous as he is, the Tale-teller cannot be wholly inconsistent; that is, he cannot at one moment espouse the cause of the Moderns, at the next that of the Ancients. A position and a point of view fairly steadily grounded are a necessary condition for the satire to operate intelligibly. (When in book three of the *Travels* Gulliver expresses contempt for the Laputans, then immediately praises them warmly, we are confused, and not in an artistic way: I would say Swift here has momentarily lost his footing.) Again, the Tale-teller cannot (except in parody, which makes it a different thing) deliver Swift's sermon on the Trinity or even the one on sleeping in church; he cannot compose *A Project for the Advancement of Religion and Reformation of Morals*. These would be gross violations of the rules because of their inappropriateness in the mouth of a maker of tubs. As soon as the Tale-teller utters his effusion to Prince Posterity, a horizon of appropriate styles and meanings is established, a system of reasonable expectations, reasonable probabilities. The horizon is wide but its exclusions are fairly clear. Among them, fundamentally, is the possibility that the Tale-teller should without warning become a non-ironical Swift—a Swift who writes straight from his convictions. The rules of the genre allow this persona occasionally to speak Swift's sentiments but only after formal provision for the shift in point of view has been made. In the midst of the Digression on Madness, for

2. E. D. Hirsch, *Validity in Interpretation* (New Haven: Yale University Press, 1967), 71ff.

example, the Tale-teller utters the purest kind of Swiftian doctrine: "For, the Brain, in its natural Position and State of Serenity, disposeth its Owner to pass his Life in the common Forms, without any Thought of subduing Multitudes to his own *Power*, his *Reasons* or his *Visions;* and the more he shapes his Understanding by the Pattern of Human Learning, the less he is inclined to form Parties after his particular Learning, the less he is inclined to form Parties after his particular Notions." The Tale-teller can legitimately speak in this way because immediately before he has made it clear that he himself is a partisan of the vapor which the world calls madness, without which we would be deprived of "those two great Blessings, *Conquests* and *Systems*," and consequently he has no love for the "common Forms." Thus the Tale-teller can utter Swift's sentiments without speaking in Swift's unmediated accents. The basic rule is that although the persona need not be a consistent character, the personation must be consistently maintained.

At a certain memorable point in the *Tale,* Swift (I think) deliberately violates the rules. The Digression on Madness divides the world in two and demands that the reader choose between them. Unlike the knight in the Wife of Bath's tale, the reader cannot refuse choice itself but must align himself with one of two intellectual-moral positions: either with happiness, delusion, credulity, the surface of things (as these are defined in the Digression), or with curiosity and officious reason which cuts and pierces and anatomizes in order to demonstrate the ugliness beneath the skin. The argument coils to its bitter climax:

> whatever Philosopher or Projector can find out an Art to sodder and patch up the Flaws and Imperfections of Nature, will deserve much better of Mankind, and teach us a more useful Science, than that so much in present Esteem, of widening and exposing them (like him who held *Anatomy* to be the ultimate End of *Physick*.) And he, whose Fortunes and Dispositions have placed him in a convenient Station to enjoy the Fruits of this noble Art; He that can with *Epicurus* content his Ideas with the *Films* and *Images* that fly off upon his Senses from the

Superficies of Things; Such a Man truly wise, creams off Nature, leaving the Sower and the Dregs, for Philosophy and Reason to lap up. This is the sublime and refined Point of Felicity, called, *the Possession of being well deceived;* The Serene Peaceful State of being a Fool among Knaves.

The shock to the reader is traumatic as he suddenly finds himself trapped in an intolerable dilemma: if he has chosen happiness and the surface of things he is a fool; if he has chosen reason he is a knave. There is no way out. No wonder he is shaken. But beyond that I think the reader has a strong sense that he has been not only trapped but booby-trapped. It is not part of the game that the Tale-teller should be able to speak in the savagely hostile accents which end the paragraph; they violate his mode of being, amorphous as it is. Instead, Swift has momentarily tossed the Tale-teller aside, speaking out in his own voice, breaking his own rules. It is as though one's chess partner suddenly reached across the board and hit one in the head with one's queen.[3]

In the passage in question the Tale-teller argues consistently for the value of happiness *("a perpetual possession of being well deceived"),* of fantasy, imagination, the surface of things. "Such a man, truly wise, creams off nature." In my view it makes no sense to say that it is the Tale-teller who in the next sentence identifies the happiness he has been praising with being "a Fool among Knaves." To be sure, throughout the *Tale* he can and does praise folly and madness—they are "good" words for him—but only in suitable contexts and with the appropriate formal insulation of meaning; here he cannot possibly be giving a favorable sense to *Fool* and *Knaves.* This would be simple incoherence, not irony; it would have the Tale-teller maintaining that true wisdom is to be a fool. There are contexts, of course, in which such a paradoxical assertion makes very good sense indeed—the wisdom of the holy fool, for example—but those

3. This momentary violation of the rules is comparable to a similar violation in the last book of *A la recherche du temps perdu,* discussed in chapter five, where Proust, not Marcel, practically shouts the name of Françoise's cousins, who live in the real world.

contexts are not invoked here. It is as though Gulliver should say, "the Houyhnhnms are wise and just creatures and should be despised." If the "Fool among Knaves" is the Tale-teller's phrase, the customary transvaluation of terms does not work; if it is Swift's phrase, however, it enacts even as it expresses his sense of the human entrapment.

That Swift should be caught in his own trap was entirely appropriate as he doubtless knew. Assuredly no fool, he was snagged by the nether jaw of the device he had set. Swift's imagery shouts his awareness of the knavish character of his own satiric procedures. Throughout the Madness section it is Reason that cuts and mangles and pierces; it is Reason that explores weak sides and publishes infirmities, that unmasks what is hidden, that exposes the flaws of Nature, that flays women and anatomizes beaux. All this bloody work is knavery, but necessary knavery; for the exercise of reason as a scalpel, with all the moral ambiguity associated with the procedure, is precisely the satirist's function. Knavery of this anatomizing kind is Swift's métier.[4]

Rawson thinks it a mistake to try to make schematic the relation between Swift and his persona, and certainly no neat system of invariant opposition will do. He thinks that despite the crushing finality of the "Fool among Knaves" the sense of the passage is left deliberately indistinct because we cannot be certain how Swift and his speaker relate. On the contrary, I think Swift's violation of the rules makes the schematism of the passage inexorable: the rhythms of the prose enforce it as does the sense. Swift imposes upon us choices ("happiness" vs. anatomizing) that are matched symmetrically by the two terms with which he springs the trap. The system is closed and out of its closure shattering energies erupt. Oddly, not all those ener-

---

4. The dissection metaphor is common in Swift. See the Drapier's characterization of William Wood's defense of his coinage as nothing more than "the last Howls of a Dog dissected alive, as I hope he hath sufficiently been." "Letter IV. To the Whole People of Ireland," *The Drapier's Letters,* in *Prose Works,* ed. Herbert Davis (Oxford: Basil Blackwell, 1941), 10:54.

gies are destructive. If, as Rawson says, the passage affirms an ancient proverb: "Knaves and fools divide the world," its brilliance is such as to assert its own kind of order in defiance of its literal message. Just as a physicist interferes with the "state of the system" when he undertakes a quantum description of a light beam, so Swift (or Pope in *The Dunciad*) alters the system of folly he is examining by giving form to his conception of it. "The wit gives pleasure in itself," says Rawson, "and playfully suggests the survival of linguistic order within a certain mental anarchy."

The issue of character arises again in a work like *A Modest Proposal*. No one would claim that the figure Swift creates to put forward the proposal is a consistent or complex or interesting person in his own fictional right. In a way the whole notion of character as applied to him seems irrelevant. In another sense, however, it is precisely our *idea* of character, and how that idea functions with respect to the projector, that controls our response to the work. Consider:

> It is a melancholly Object to those, who walk through this great Town, or travel in the Country; when they see the *Streets,* the *Roads,* and *Cabbin-doors* crowded with *Beggars* of the Female Sex, followed by three, four, or six Children, *all in Rags,* and importuning every Passenger for an Alms. These *Mothers,* instead of being able to work for their honest Livelyhood, are forced to employ all their Time in stroling to beg Sustenance for their *helpless Infants;* who, as they grow up, either turn *Thieves* for want of Work; or leave their *dear Native Country, to fight for the Pretender in* Spain, or sell themselves to the *Barbadoes.*

Swift plays upon what he knows will be the reader's assumptions about the kind of man who can speak so sympathetically of the Irish condition. Given the conventions of character depiction, only that slight intimation is necessary to establish in the reader's mind a formidable set of expectations about what can and cannot follow from such an introduction. These are the expectations that Swift manipulates with such extraordinary results.

Although a tool of the satiric fiction, the persona of *A Modest Proposal* is bound by the same minimal generic rules that govern the spokesman of *A Tale of a Tub;* that is, he cannot contradict himself haphazardly, he cannot speak in Swift's unmediated voice. Nevertheless, that voice comes through once or twice in defiance of the rules. One advantage the projector sees in his cannibalistic proposal is that it will not disoblige England: "For, this Kind of Commodity will not bear Exportation; the Flesh being of too tender a Consistence, to admit a long Continuance in Salt; *although, perhaps, I could name a Country, which would be glad to eat up our whole Nation without it.*" The last part of the sentence is unmistakably not the projector but Swift himself. Whereas in *A Tale of a Tub* Swift's intervention produces a shattering experience for the reader, here the unsignaled shift in tone disturbs him momentarily if at all. An English reader in Swift's day would doubtless have responded to the intrusion much more intensely. It all depends on who the victim is.

The identification of victims of Swift's satire is no longer as simple as once it was, the catalogue having been expanded by recent criticism far beyond obvious targets to include the reader—all readers—and, as we saw in chapter six, Swift himself. On the face of it, such identifications are startling, for they radically violate received notions about satire's aims and function, matters on which Swift's official ideas at least, are as conventional as his ideas on religion. "There are two Ends that Men propose in writing Satyr; one of them less noble than the other, as regarding nothing further than the private Satisfaction, and Pleasure of the Writer; but without any View towards *personal Malice:* The other is a *publick Spirit,* prompting Men of *Genius* and Virtue, to mend the World as far as they are able." The satirist effects this noble end by laughing men out of their follies and vices. It is one of the pattest formulas of self-justification in the lexicon and one of the least examined. Swift puts the formula under some pressure, as we shall see, but never, I think, to the point where his own role as satirist is seriously in question. His aligning himself in the passage above with men of "*Genius* and Virtue" hardly shows him as a conscious victim of his own ridicule. As for the generality of readers as victims, the discussion of the range and effect of satire in the Preface to the *Tale of a Tub* shows Swift acutely aware of the weakness in indiscriminate attack: "Satyr being levelled at all, is never resented for an offense by any, since every individual Person makes bold to understand it of others, and very wisely removes his particular Part of the Burthen upon the shoulders of the World, which are broad enough, and able to bear it." The argument for individual, local satire, as opposed to that which inveighs against mankind, is explicit and pointed: the satirist's proper target is "*such a one* [who] starved half the Fleet," not "People in general." Obviously, Swift does not stick to his own prescription: he attacks individuals, professions, institutions, creeds—in the Digression on Madness he involves the world. Our question is whether (except in the last instance and perhaps one or two others) the reader, however remote he may be from the obvious targets, is himself victimized by the satire—whether, as Rawson puts it, his escape routes are closed. And then, to what degree is Swift himself, rather than his persona, involved.[5]

Satire is purportedly written to two audiences: in one are the guilty and those most likely to be infected by the guilty, in the other "all right-thinking men," or, as Swift says, "*a great majority among the Men of Tast,*" who share the author's view and values. This latter group, although sometimes in danger of ricochets, is unlikely to be brought under direct fire, most obviously because it forms a friendly camp and is presumably untainted by the vice or folly under examination. The satirist normally arranges things so that the object of his attack is definable against the background of what that object is not: Wotton is defined by contrast with Sir William Temple (clearly a Man of Tast), dissenting Jack by contrast with Martin, who, we are

5. Swift's characterization of satire is in *Prose Works,* 12:34.

told, represents the *"most perfect"* of all churches in *"Discipline and Doctrine."* A Tale of a Tub provides a surprising number of such positives for the reader to cling to: the coats, of course (i.e., *"the Doctrine and Faith of Christianity by the Wisdom of the Divine Founder fitted to all Times, Places and Circumstances"*) and Martin, but positives also in the Digressions. Those of us who write on Swift doubtless take heart from the knowledge that at one happy time in the world's history there were critics other than that formidable race descended from the union of Momus and Hybris, who begat Zoilus. One group of critics used to restore ancient learning from the ravages of time and neglect; another group "invented or drew up rules for themselves and the World, by observing which, a careful Reader might be able to pronounce upon the productions of the *Learned,* form his Taste to a true Relish of the *Sublime* and the *Admirable,* and divide every Beauty of Matter or Style from the Corruption that Apes it." Although these critics have long been extinct, we are told, each of us must feel that somehow we are the true heirs. How else could we write?

Even in fiercer passages of the satires—those that seem to be torn from the nightmares that tormented Swift—there is likely to be formal provision for a way out. One of his worst fears was certainly, as Empson says, that religion may be no more than a perversion of sexuality, a thesis propounded in great detail by Swift's spokesman in the *Mechanical Operation of the Spirit.* So brilliant and so shocking is this exposition that one forgets the ways to transcendence, other than the mechanical way, mentioned in the text: inspiration from God, possession by the devil, natural causes such as imagination, grief, pain. Swift has no more interest in discussing these legitimate ways of transporting the soul beyond matter than, as a clergyman, he has in discussing the doctrine of the Trinity; but their presence in his text is a necessary element freeing his subversive imagination to show how the spirit may be improved by belching or by prudent management of syphilitic infection, giving him and us, at least in formal terms, a way out.[6]

6. See his sermon on the Trinity, in *Prose Works,* 11:159–68.

This is a characteristic mark of Swift; it is his way of exercising what Murray Krieger calls the classic vision. Swift entertains the possibility that the structures which order reality, whether those of reason or religion, may be mere projections of our minds, desperate but factitious attempts to impose order on what is ineluctably chaos. He fantasizes himself into the skins of those who represent horror to him most fully—a Lord Wharton, a madman—or of those who must face head-on what he fears—a Gulliver. Through their eyes and in their voices he confronts the extreme: confronts but does not embrace. The extreme is there, invoked by the violence of thought and metaphor, but rejected at the same time by the formal ordering of his work, by the paths he leaves open.[7]

Many readers, to be sure, find that *Gulliver's Travels* blocks all escape routes; and, clearly, if Gulliver's "All men are yahoos" is Swift's last word, then the closure of the system is complete. To read the *Travels* this way, however, is to conclude that in Swift's view no moral distinction can be made between Dr. Arbuthnot and Lord Wharton, between Sir Thomas More and Henry VIII, between Stella and Mrs. Manley. All are equally loathsome brutes, and Swift is brutish among them. I find the reading incredible, ignoring as it does the possibilities of a reasonable society adumbrated in Brobdingnag, of a decent life shown in Don Pedro. In literature Don Pedro serves Swift as an escape from Yahoodom, just as in life John, Peter, Thomas, and Councillor Such-a-One (whom Swift told Pope he dearly loved) served as an escape from total misanthropy. Don Pedro provides a way out.[8]

Thus I think it a mistake to read Swift's satire as though it were all one vast "Fool among Knaves" trap into which reader and author fall together. It is glib to say that we are all involved in all the vices that satire attacks—that we are all Lord Whartons or John Duntons or whatever, and it is a flaccid morality that

7. Murray Krieger, *The Classic Vision* (Baltimore: Johns Hopkins University Press, 1971), 255–69.

8. Swift, *Correspondence,* ed. Harold Williams, 5 vols. (Oxford: Clarendon Press, 1963–65), 3:103.

refuses to discriminate. On the other hand, the escape routes which make discrimination possible are ill-marked in Swift's work, obscure and easy to overlook altogether—a very different situation from that in Pope who emphatically draws the distinction between the righteous and the wicked. Swift's assaults generate such an overplus of energy, they come from so many directions with such unexpected vehemence and wit that ways out are likely to be forgotten as the reader is enveloped by the storm. Rawson is splendid on this. He speaks of how the sudden intensity of a sentence like "Last Week I saw a Woman *flay'd,* and you will hardly believe, how much it altered her Person for the worse," not only serves the argument it illustrates but spills over the surrounding context: the energies of the sentence are in excess of the demands of the logic. This spill-over phenomenon, Rawson says, is characteristic of Swift's style; it contributes to the reader's sense of impasse, of unease, to the feeling that he is somehow catching the hostility meant for someone else.[9]

This seems to me an important insight into the way Swift's prose works. At one point or another in his satire we all recognize aspects of ourselves in the object of ridicule; if we don't we are either hypocrites or poor readers. On the other hand, we are also conscious of being battered even when free of guilt; attacks on abuses in which we as individuals can have no conceivable part hurt, not because of our complicity, but simply as a result of the overplus of hostility in the air. Normal identification with the satirist and its attendant invulnerability, although possible at a formal, rational level, is hopelessly disturbed by the dangerous charges of animus flying about. My impression is, however, that in these instances the reader feels attacked—as though someone has hit him from a dark corner—rather than made to feel guilty. Rawson writes: "Where the aggression turns indistinct, and overspills the area of specifiable moral guilt, no opportunity is given for complacent self-exculpation on a specific front, and the reader becomes implicated. Instead of permitting the individual to shift his load onto the world's shoulders, Swift forces the

9. Rawson, *Gulliver and the Gentle Reader,* 33ff.

reader to carry the world's load on *his.*" But I doubt that it is *guilt* the reader feels about the woman flayed; he is not in fact guilty of the flaying, nor is he likely to feel the same equanimity before the image of horror that Swift's spokesman exhibits— surely a matter for guilt. If the reader recognizes that, like the Tale-teller, he sometimes treats people as things, or that he lives complacently in a society that endorses unspeakable cruelties, the vaguely guilty twinges accompanying these reflections are low-order responses compared to the shock he gets from the sentence, the battering he undergoes from the spill-over of negative emotion. At the same time, as Irvin Ehrenpreis points out, the reader may experience an illicit joy (for which he may feel guilt) that a man could write such a "beautiful" sentence.[10]

In analyzing the overspill phenomenon, Rawson is pointing to real effects in Swift's satire that run counter to the formal ordering of things. These are subjective matters, impossible to specify precisely or measure accurately; but I think the analysis goes a long way toward accounting for the feelings of unjustified victimization likely to result from a bout with Swift. The danger of concentrating too exclusively on these effects is that we may be led to read all Swift's satire as though it were the climactic passage of the Digression on Madness. Not even Swift's work can live consistently at that heat.

In the preceding chapter I tried to define my sense of the degree to which Swift, through his persona, expresses his own complicity in the madness and the badness that he exposes; here I want to explore self-reflexive implications of Swift's frequently expressed distrust of his own medium. In the Apology to *A Tale of a Tub* Swift, speaking in his own person, affirms and reaffirms the traditional justifications of satire: gross corruptions in religion and learning can best be eliminated by satire's cleansing action. On the other hand, in the Preface to the same work, he (or, as I prefer, his persona) launches a brilliantly destructive foray—a satirical foray—against the practice of satire itself. Satirists lash vices, says the Tale-teller, but with pathetic futility; for

10. Ehrenpreis, "Swift and the Comedy of Evil," 213–19.

"there is not, through all Nature, another so callous and insensible a Member as the *World's Posteriors.*" Satirists' attacks on avarice and hypocrisy are meaningless: " 'Tis but a *Ball* bandied to and fro, and every Man carries a *Racket* about Him to strike it from himself among the rest of the Company." If satirists dare to expose the villainy of individual persons, they only invite persecution. This attack on satire is managed with a great flurry of denigratory imagery, in one paragraph satirists being compared with flogging pedants, nettles, weeds, thistles, their wit with dull razors and rotten teeth. The "Satyrical Itch" is a disease.

In an interesting analysis of these matters, Gardner Stout, Jr., reads the relevant passages of *A Tale of a Tub* as Swift's own admission that satire serves no useful purpose. "Though he finds Alecto's whip a congenial instrument for scourging fools, he recognizes that, in lashing the world with wit and humor to mend it, his satire is impotent, partly because those it strikes are temperamentally disqualified from feeling it by the very vices for which they are satirized." Stout finds Swift condemning his own motives and procedures: like the True Critic, the Satirist—Swift included—is a collector of mankind's faults, which become distilled into his own person. The satirist messes about in the ordure of human nature, as much a part of the Bedlamite world he describes as any committed lunatic. According to this reading, Swift sees himself as implicated in all that he attacks even as he recognizes that the attack itself is impotent. Here, from some cosmic perspective, the satirist is indeed satirized.[11]

But is it so? The expressed distrust of satire is unmistakable, the only question being whether Swift's own satire comes within the orbit of critique. The whole passage in the Preface is framed by an elaborate disclaimer from the Tale-teller: " 'Tis a great Ease to my Conscience that I have writ so elaborate and useful a Discourse without one grain of Satyr intermixt; which is the sole point wherein I have taken leave to dissent from the

---

11. Stout, "Speaker and Satiric Vision in Swift's *Tale of a Tub,*" 186.

famous Originals of our Age and Country." If the Tale-teller dissents from the Originals, then Swift, following the rules of the rhetorical game, can legitimately attack them through the mouth of his persona: hence the denigratory images. The sentence about the world's posteriors sounds like Swift, but the sentiments are those of a hundred earlier satirists, who have rarely had many illusions about their real power to effect reform. Besides, Swift's target here is the spate of satire in the 1690s which so offended Sir William Temple, the satire to which Aesop refers when, speaking with Swift's authority in the *Battle of the Books,* he asserts that the only genuine production of the Moderns is *"a large Vein of Wrangling and Satyr, much of a Nature and Substance with the* Spider's *Poison."* To attack *that* satire is by no means the same as attacking satire itself.

Furthermore, an odd paradox obtains whereby to admit that satire has little or no effect on a guilty audience is to reinforce the satirical attack. Yeats once thought that Wyndham Lewis's *Apes of God* would shake up London literary society. But Lewis disagreed: "Nothing could change the kind of people of whom I wrote—they had not the necessary vitality for that." The confession of futility turns into the ultimate put-down. Whether that, in turn, has effect is, of course, open to the same doubt as before. Swift's best-known statement questioning the efficacy of satire is in the Preface to the *Battle of the Books.* Here he speaks in his own person, as the author, not in the guise of a muddle-headed modern: *"Satyr is a sort of Glass, wherein Beholders do generally discover every body's Face but their Own; which is the chief Reason for that kind Reception it meets in the World and that so very few are offended with it."* Although this wryly admits that most satire does not get home to those for whom it is intended, that fact itself condemns those who look in the glass: they wilfully refuse to see their own images and either stupidly or hypocritically welcome what exposes their folly. An admission of satiric futility here is overborn by the attack, which in the following sentences escalates into a most unpleasant threat that the wit of the satirist's opponent will end up as something fit only to be thrown to the hogs. The truculence of this satirist has nothing to do with impotence: these teeth can bite.[12]

Interesting logical issues arise when, as in the Preface to *A Tale of a Tub,* a satirist satirizes satire. Wyndham Lewis involves himself in this situation in a very Swiftian way in his novel *Apes of God.* Horace Zagreus, who speaks for Lewis, uses Swift's imagery: "'How is it that no one ever sees *himself* in the public mirror?'" The world, he concludes, is hopelessly past mending:

> "People feel themselves under the special protection of the author when they read a satire on their circle—am I right!...
> It is always the *other fellows* (never them) that their accredited romancer is depicting, for their sport.... At all events nothing happens. It would seem that it is impossible to devise anything sufficiently cruel for the rhinoceros hides grown by a civilized man and a civilized woman.... It is almost as if, when they saw him approaching, they exclaimed: '*Here comes a good satirist! We'll give him some sport. We are just the sort of animals he loves.*' Then the official satirist fills his pages with monsters and a sprinkling of rather sentimental 'personnages sympathiques,' and everybody is perfectly happy. The satirist is, of course, quite as insensitive as his subjects, as a rule. Nothing really disgusts him."

This satirical denigration of both the function of satire and the character of the satirist comes in the midst of one of the fiercest satirical novels ever written. Is Lewis victimized by his own attack? Only in the most remote way, I should think. Satire about satire is like thinking about thought, or communication about communication: as Bertrand Russell made clear, in his theory of logical types, different logical orders are involved and should not be confused. The satirical attacks on satire of both Lewis and Swift are launched from levels higher than their object. This is metasatire, and according to the rules of this game the position of the authors is privileged. Except for nonlogical effects of the kind Rawson discusses, they escape their own critique.[13]

12. Wyndham Lewis, *Rude Assignment* (London: Hutchinson, 1950), 201.
13. Wyndham Lewis, *Apes of God* (Baltimore: Penguin, 1965), 268. As for the paradox of the satirist satirizing satire, it is of the order of the ancient "liar"

On January 11, 1710–11, Swift recorded in the *Journal to Stella*
that he was setting up his protégé, "little" Harrison, as the new
Tatler, Richard Steele having given up the journal. On March 14
he writes: "little Harrison the Tatler came to me, and begged me
to dictate a paper to him, which I was forced in charity to do."
Next day the *Tatler* appeared, lauding old times when men of
wit had power: "The Hopes of being celebrated, or the Dread
of being stigmatized, procured an universal Respect and Awe"
for the poets. Swift's bias is revealed when he cites Aretino as the
great example: all the princes of Europe trembled lest they be
pilloried in his satire. A week later in another paper (also attributed to Swift) Isaac Bickerstaff playfully identifies himself as one
who, in accordance with Pythagorean doctrine, was born centuries ago and has lived through many incarnations. At one
time, Bickerstaff says in this metempsychic version of persona
theory, he was the leading wit of France, at another time had a
statue erected to him in Italy; and when he came to England at
the end of the seventeenth century he entered the body of the
most talented man of letters there—a man easily identified as
Jonathan Swift. The common element in Isaac Bickerstaff's incarnations, he tells us, is that "I have in every one of them
opposed my self with the utmost Resolution to the Follies and
Vices of the several Ages I have been acquainted with, that I have
often rallied the World into good Manners, and kept the greatest
Princes in Awe of my Satyr."[14]

The battered reader of his work finds it pleasant to see Swift
relaxing into fantasy, playing the role of satirist-hero: slaying

---

paradox: Epimenides the Cretan said that all Cretans are liars, or of Bertrand
Russell's paradox of the class of all classes not belonging to themselves. For
Russell's solution—or as W. V. Quine puts it, his parrying of the paradoxes by
way of his theory of a hierarchical order of logical types—see *Principia Mathemat-
ica*, with Alfred North Whitehead, 3 vols., 2d ed. (Cambridge: Cambridge University Press, 1935), 1:60ff. Quine's characterization is in "Russell's Ontologial
Development," *Bertrand Russell: Philosopher of the Century* (London: George
Allen and Unwin, 1967), 307. An excellent discussion of some of these matters
appears in the chapter "Paradoxical Communication" in Paul Watzlawick and
others, *Pragmatics of Human Communication* (New York: W. W. Norton, 1967),
187–229.

14. Swift, *Prose Works*, 2:257–63. For the attribution, see Herbert Davis's
Introduction to the volume, xxxv–xxxvi.

dragons, rescuing princesses, laughing the world into civility.
It is one of many images of the satirist in his work, from the
rotten-toothed mumbler of the *Tale,* through the bloody anato-
mist and the culture hero to the derisive Jove of the poem
"The Day of Judgment." In that nightmare vision Jove lays bare
hypocrisy, exposes secret pride and mean motives—acts, in
short, as a satirist; acts, as Lord Chesterfield said, like Voltaire:

> With a Whirl of Thought oppress'd,
> I sink from Reverie to Rest.
> An horrid Vision seiz'd my Head,
> I saw the Graves give up their Dead.
> Jove, arm'd with Terrors, burst the Skies,
> And Thunder roars, and Light'ning flies!
> Amaz'd, confus'd, its Fate unknown,
> The World stands trembling at his Throne.
> While each pale Sinner hangs his Head,
> Jove, nodding, shook the Heav'ns, and said,
> "Offending Race of Human Kind,
> By Nature, Reason, Learning, blind;
> You who thro' Frailty step'd aside,
> And you who never fell—*thro' Pride;*
> You who in different Sects have shamm'd,
> And come to see each other damn'd;
> (So some Folks told you, but they knew
> No more of Jove's Designs than you)
> The World's mad Business now is o'er,
> And I resent these Pranks no more.
> I to such Blockheads set my Wit!
> I damn such Fools!—Go, go, you're bit."[15]

As part of the "Offending Race of Human Kind" Swift is
damned with the rest, but his major identification is clearly with
the satirist-god of the vision. In public apologiae Swift asserted
the conventional moral justification of the satirist; in private he
battled the doubts that assailed him, expressing some of those

15. *The Poems of Jonathan Swift,* ed. Harold Williams, 3 vols. (Oxford: Clarendon Press, 1958), 2:578–79.

doubts indirectly by way of the Tale-teller and others of his erratic personae; but in the compensatory mode of fantasy, and speaking through the most congenial persona of all, Swift lays claim to mythical powers.

"My Lord," wrote Swift in *A Letter Concerning the Weavers*, "I freely own it a wild Imagination that any words will cure the sottishness of men or the vanity of women . . . ," but the confession of futility becomes the springboard of attack as he pushes forward his argument with a caustic jibe. Whatever doubts Swift entertained about satire, he never allowed them to interfere with his métier. That he explored to the limit.

8 The Presentation of Self in Doggerel Rhyme

According to Michael Shinagel's *Concordance,* the first person singular pronoun appears 1503 times in Swift's poems. It is the eighth most frequently used word, outnumbered only by articles, conjunctions, prepositions—*the, and, to, a,* and the like—and, perhaps surprisingly, by the pronoun *his* (1604 appearances). *His,* however, is often associated with the word *Dean,* which is the second most frequently used noun in the poems (164 appearances). Most of the time, of course, *Dean* is a third-person reference to Jonathan Swift himself; that is, the word *Dean* is a dramatized version of the first person pronoun. Thus *his,* which outnumbers *I,* is often a satellite of the third person form of *I* with the result that by all odds the most frequently used significant words in Swift's poetry refer in some sense to Swift himself.

There are no surprises here; the statistical data only support every reader's impression that Jonathan Swift permeates the poems—we are closer to him here, Sir Harold Williams, Swift's great editor, thinks than in the whole body of the prose. F. Elrington Ball claims that in his verse Swift "sets forth his life as in a panorama, he shows more clearly than in his prose his peculiar turn of thought, and he reveals his character in all its phases." This feeling, which we are all likely to share, is certainly correlated with the abundant use Swift makes of himself as subject and as object in the poems.[1]

Even as we say this, however, we recall how tricky it is to cope with Swift's use of the first person pronoun in his prose satires, in *A Tale of a Tub,* for example:

> In my Disposure of Employments of the Brain, I have thought fit to make *Invention* the *Master,* and to give *Method* and *Reason,* the Office of its *Lacquays.* The Cause of this Distribution was, from observing it my peculiar Case, to be often under a Temptation of being *Witty,* upon Occasions, where I could be neither *Wise* nor *Sound,* nor any thing to the Matter in hand. And, I am too much a Servant of the *Modern* Way, to neglect any such Opportunities, whatever Pains or Improprieties I may be at, to introduce them. (Conclusion, 209)

To what degree can this be taken as a "serious" comment on the composition of the *Tale,* as another version of the Apology? Is it consciously self-referential, Swift deliberately associating himself with fatuities that he normally ridicules? If it is not self-referential, why does he use the first person? The poetry presents problems of similar complexity although formally they are often somewhat different. True, Swift sometimes personates a loathed object in the poems, just as he does in prose, raising interpretive problems of precisely the same order. In the poem "Toland's Invitation to Dismal," for example, Swift takes on the character and speaks in the voice of the hated John Toland, the deist, who in the poem invites Dismal (that is, Lord Nottingham) to celebrate the anniversary of Charles I's execution.

> If, dearest *Dismal,* you for once can Dine
> Upon a single Dish, and Tavern Wine . . .
> To morrow We our *Mystick Feast* prepare,
> Where Thou, our latest Proselyte, shalt share:

---

1. Williams, Introduction to *Poems of Jonathan Swift,* 1:xlvi. Swift's poems are cited from this edition (see chap. 7, n. 15 above). References to volume and page are given in the text.

> When We, by proper Signs and Symbols tell,
> How, by *Brave Hands,* the *Royal Traytor* fell;
> The Meat shall represent the *Tyrant's* Head,
> The Wine, his Blood, *our Predecessors* shed. (1:162)

The situation is thus precisely the same as that in the prose *Letter of Thanks from My Lord Wharton* in which Swift insinuates himself into the skin, and speaks through the mouth, of the infamous Wharton. In both instances the reader must decide to what degree, if any, Swift's use of the first person pronoun, his assumed identification with the person we know he is attacking, brings Swift within the orbit of his own satire. Does his writing "I" in poem or in prose somehow imply his own complicity in Toland's or Wharton's evil? As we have seen, some distinguished critics of our day—Irvin Ehrenpreis most notably—think that it does. I made my disagreement with that position clear in chapter six and shall not pursue the matter further here.

Instead, I want to look at some complications that arise when Swift presents himself in the poems as an object of contemplation and discussion: Swift on "Swift"—or is it "Swift" on "Swift"? Can we ever dispense with the quotation marks? W. B. Carnochan asks. It is useful to distinguish such poems from those which, though written in the first person, may be said to reveal rather than present Swift. I think of the early Odes: for example, a heated description in the "Ode to Sir William Temple" of his struggles with what he calls his "(almost) Virgin-Muse." Swift complains of Nature's cruelty:

> Some she condemns for Life to try
> To dig the leaden Mines of deep Philosophy:
> Me she has to the Muse's Gallies ty'd,
> In vain I try to cross this spacious Main,
>   In vain I tug and pull the Oar,
>   And when I almost reach the Shore
> Strait the Muse turns the Helm, and I launch out
>   again . . . (1:32)

We feel that we are very close to the young Swift in passages like these: close to the rawness of his ambition, the pain of his frustrations, poetic and otherwise. Authentic as it may be, however, the romantic image of the writer we get from the Odes is an involuntary one, a long remove from the complex image we are offered in the later, deliberately self-referential verses.

In an influential essay called "Makers and Persons" Patrick Cruttwell insists on the significance of the truism that makers *are* persons: the only source of the maker's material is himself; he is, necessarily, something of an exhibitionist. Cruttwell lists several strategies governing the ways the exhibition can be performed:

1. The Direct: what purports to be a simple transcript from person to maker; a presentation of self untouched, undisguised, as in confessions, autobiography. But every writer "makes," says Cruttwell, even as he professes merely to record.

2. The Masked: "the making of a self which pretends not to be, but which encourages the reader to think it is, the person of the writer"; for example, Conrad's creation of Marlowe, Sterne's of Tristram and Yorick.

3. The Mythologized: a presentation of self which transposes the person into a symbolic figure or reference; "the more these mythologised self-presentations repudiate interpretation in terms of the person," says Cruttwell, "the more . . . they receive it."

4. The Dramatized: here the distance is greatest between person and maker, as with Swift's poem "Toland's Invitation to Dismal." The person is there, inevitably, but remote, entering the work only as a kind of "leakage."[2]

Cruttwell's third category, the Mythologized, fits most of the major poems in which Swift uses himself as subject. That is, Swift presents himself in these poems in such a way that he is transformed into a symbolic figure: into the archetypal figure of the Satirist. Consider "An Epistle to a Lady Who desired the Author to make Verses on Her in the Heroick Stile," not one of Swift's best-known, but surely one of his most extraordinary, poems—at once a splendid example of his use of raillery, of

2. Patrick Cruttwell, "Makers and Persons," *Hudson Review* 12 (1959–60): 487–97; cf. William K. Wimsatt, "Genesis: An Argument Resumed," in his *Day of the Leopards* (Yale University Press, 1976), 11ff.

praise-by-blame, as he lovingly teases Lady Acheson; of his most daring satire against King George and Walpole's government (the poem caused the arrest of Swift's printer and bookseller, and Walpole was prepared to arrest Swift himself but backed down when told it would take an army of 10,000 men to arrest the Dean in Ireland); and one of the best examples of Swift's defense of his practice as satirist. The first half of the poem is an engaging dialogue between the Dean and his "pupil," Lady Acheson. The Dean manages his customary moral instruction with exemplary delicacy; the Lady spiritedly defends herself against his accusations and enters a plea:

> But, I beg, suspend a While,
> That same paultry *Burlesque* Stile:
> Drop, for once, your constant Rule,
> Turning all to Ridicule. . . .
>
> Sing my Praise in Strain sublime:
> Treat me not with Doggrel Rhime. (2:631)

In the second half of the poem the Dean justifies his ungrateful art. As to style, the Heroick Strain is not for him:

> I, as all the Parish knows,
> Hardly can be grave in Prose:
> Still to lash, and lashing Smile,
> Ill befits a lofty Stile.
> From the Planet of my Birth,
> I encounter Vice with Mirth.
> Wicked Ministers of State
> I can easier scorn than hate:
> And I find it answers right:
> Scorn torments them more than Spight. (2:634)

This is very much like Horace disavowing the grand style, as in *Satires* four and ten of the first Book he tries to create his own space in relation to his great predecessor, Lucilius—a splendid example, by the way, of an early working out of the anxiety of influence. Horace's laughter at evildoers, he asserts, is couched in unpretentious verse, unworthy to be called poetry at all. He avoids the fierce Lucilian mode, which makes people fear the satirist. There is no malice in him; he simply has to have his laugh out at the idiocies he sees around him. Besides, a mocking laugh or ridicule often does the job better than grave reproof—the famous *ridiculum acri/fortius,* etc. Or, as Swift puts it in his doggerel way:

> Ridicule has greater Pow'r
> To reform the World, than Sour.

Or again:

> Horses thus, let Jockeys judge else,
> Switches better guide than Cudgels. (2:636)

The other Horatian themes are in Swift too; in short, we are presented in the "Epistle to a Lady" with a Horace redivivus. Swift's claim to the role is bolstered as he offers us a model of his satiric practice, his treatment of Lady Acheson in the very poem we are reading:

> Thus, I find it by Experiment,
> Scolding moves you less than Merriment

—moral merriment of the kind we have experienced in the first 130 lines of the poem; the same kind of merriment Swift professes to be motivated by when he has

> a Fling
> Both at Senate-House, and [King]...
> As my Method of Reforming,
> Is by Laughing, not by Storming. (2:636–37)

Alongside these professions of Horatian urbanity, however, are examples of another kind of Swiftian satire: small explosions violating completely the stylistic and tonal claims that have just been made:

> Safe within my little Wherry,
> All their Madness makes me merry:

> Like the Watermen of *Thames,*
> I row by, and call them Names.
> Like the ever-laughing Sage,
> In a Jest I spend my Rage:
> (Tho' it must be understood,
> I would hang them if I cou'd.) (2:635)

Although the catharsis theme intimated here might be considered properly Horatian, neither the name-calling, boatman style, nor the confession of rage can be considered within the Horatian range; and the last couplet about hanging makes a mockery of Swift's claims to be amusedly above the battle. Parenthetically, to be tempted into reading that couplet as a genial exaggeration is surely a mistake. During his years of power in London, Swift once intervened in the case of a rapist who, after having been condemned to be hanged, was about to be pardoned. Swift had the pardon squelched. "'Tis true," he writes in the *Journal to Stella* (July 25, 1711), "the fellow had lain with her a hundred times before; but what care I for that? What! must a woman be ravished because she is a whore? . . . besides, he was a fiddler, and consequently a rogue, and deserved hanging for something else; and so he shall swing." Under those rules Walpole would be lucky to get off with hanging.

A second outburst in the poem reverts to the flailing kind of satire associated with Lucilius, the kind Horace specifically disavows:

> Let me, tho' the Smell be Noisom,
> Strip their Bums; let CALEB hoyse 'em;
> Then, apply ALECTO's Whip,
> Till they wriggle, howl, and skip.

Swift is aware of incongruity here; at least he has Lady Acheson voice some sense of it:

> Deuce is in you Mr. Dean;
> What can all this Passion mean? (2:635)

But the recognition is momentary as the Dean reasserts his claim that he writes in the Horatian mode.

Erving Goffman says that on certain occasions a performer "may be taken in by his own act, convinced at the moment that the impression of reality which he fosters is the one and only reality." As we shall see, Swift was, like Pope, sometimes taken in by his own act, but probably not here; the countersignals are too blatant. Instead of a situation in which we see Swift playing the role of Horatian satirist, but playing it ineptly because the performance includes out-of-character material, I think we have Swift playing at playing the role. In Goffman's terms, Swift shows us the "backstage" of the performance, "Where the impression fostered by the performance is knowingly contradicted." In effect Swift laughs at his own presentation of himself. The self-mockery leaves the contradiction unresolved; that is, Swift's claim to Horatian urbanity and restraint and his simultaneous recognition of the rage that actually moves him confront each other in stark opposition. The self-mockery is simple recognition of that fact. It is the kind of self-mockery that goes with his frequently-expressed distrust of satire as a reforming instrument: *"Satyr is a sort of Glass, wherein Beholders do generally discover every body's Face but their Own."* The version of this antinomy in the "Epistle to a Lady" goes this way. Lady Acheson speaks:

> Drop, for once, your constant Rule,
> Turning all to Ridicule:
> Teaching others how to ape ye;
> Court, nor Parli'ment, can 'scape ye;
> Treat the Publick, and your Friends,
> Both alike; while neither mends. (2:631)

The accusation, Swift making it through the mouth of Lady Acheson against himself, is unanswered and unanswerable; and Swift's whole career is undercut.[3]

A final touch: the very style in which the poet presents himself constitutes a kind of self-mockery:

> Sing my Praise in Strain sublime:
> Treat me not with Doggrel Rhime, (2:631)

3. Goffman, *The Presentation of Self in Everyday Life,* 80, 112.

Lady Acheson begs, fully aware of the principles of stylistic decorum. There is a sense in which the satirist Swift might be said to be begging with her; for the statement of his case as satirist, the presentation he makes of himself, can be taken seriously only when put forward in a style worthy of a serious occasion. It is Horace's dilemma exacerbated. But Swift—this Swift—can no more treat himself in "lofty Numbers" than he can treat Lady Acheson; were he to try, he says, he would burst like a rocket:

> All my *Fire* would fall in Scraps. (2:638)

So despite Lady Acheson's plea the doggerel mode prevails with all the belittling (and self-belittling) effects she has foreseen. By one of the oddities of rhetorical discourse, however, the self-belittling turns out to have positive advantages for the poet and the self he is presenting. It makes acceptable the self-praise lying at the heart of the poem, which if offered straight on would violate our sense of the appropriate, but tempered by the mock modesty of the doggerel style wins our sympathy. As Dr. Johnson says, "all censure of a man's self is oblique self-praise." Swift manages the obliquity in the "Epistle to a Lady" in such a way as to achieve one of his most engaging self-portraits. He was sixty-six years old when he wrote it.

Without some device of obliquity of this sort Swift's poems on himself can be downright embarrassing. "The Author upon Himself" (1714), written in the third person as though from an objective point of view, is straight self-justification. Although he claims in the poem that "Humour and Mirth had Place in all he writ," Swift can produce utterly humorless passages like the following:

> And now, the publick Int'rest to support,
> By *Harley S[wift]* invited comes to Court.
> In Favour grows with Ministers of State;
> Admitted private, when Superiors wait:
> And, *Harley,* not asham'd his Choice to own,
> Takes him to *Windsor* in his Coach, alone.
> At *Windsor S[wift]* no sooner can appear,

> But *St. John* comes and whispers in his Ear;
> The Waiters stand in Ranks; the Yeomen cry,
> *Make Room;* as if a Duke were passing by. (1:194)

Just as there is no irony here, no indirection, so there are no
doggerel rhymes, no jogging tetrameter; instead a straight pen-
tameter couplet, regular and unadventurous, making an appropriate vehicle for what seems to be an instance of Cruttwell's
"direct transcript" from person—one aspect of the person—to
maker: Swift at his most intolerable.

"A Panegyric on the Reverend Dean Swift" (1730), which
sounds as though it might be in the same mode, actually goes
well beyond obliquity: Swift claims that it is a presentation of
his anti-self. The poem is a libel on Swift written by Swift himself. He explains this oddity in a letter to Lord Bathurst:

> Having some months ago much & often offended the ruling
> party, and often worried by libellers I am at the pains of
> writing one in their style & manner, & sent it by an unknown
> hand to a Whig printer who very faithfully published it. I took
> special care to accuse myself but of one fault of which I am
> really guilty . . . but with the rest of the Satyr I chose to abuse
> myself with the direct reverse of my character.

He writes in the same vein to John Gay, confessing that he was
the author of a "Scrubb libel," written in the "style & Genius of
such scoundrels," against himself. The "Panegyric on the Reverend Dean Swift" is a very strange performance, a vivid example of Swift's masochistic compulsion to pick at his own sores.
Echoing actual attacks made on him over the years, it is written
as though by Swift's friend Patrick Delaney in a sadistic mood,
or perhaps by an enemy pretending to be Delaney; in any event
it is written with the intent of hurting Jonathan Swift.[4]

4. Although both Elrington Ball and Sir Harold Williams, the authorities in
these matters, attribute the "Panegyric" to Swift, George Faulkner, Swift's
Dublin publisher, assigned the poem to a Grub Street writer named James Arbuckle. Recently the bibliographer D. F. Foxon found a copy of a London
edition of the "Panegyric" "bound in a collection of Arbuckle's published
poems" (*English Verse, 1701–1750*, 2 vols. [Cambridge: Cambridge University

A brief bit of background is necessary. A few months before publication of the "Panegyric" Swift had written a poem called "A Libel on Dr. Delaney," containing a savagely bitter attack on patrons and those who sell themselves to benefit from patronage:

> For, as their Appetites to quench,
> Lords keep a Pimp to bring a Wench;
> So, Men of Wit are but a kind
> Of Pandars to a vicious Mind,
> Who proper Objects must provide
> To gratify their Lust of Pride. (2:480)

He lists examples, with details, of writers who have been such panders and who have been shabbily treated by patrons: Congreve, Steele, Gay, Addison. Pope is singled out as the great exception: his translation of Homer made him financially independent; his great heart would never permit him "To lick a *Rascal Statesman's Spittle*" (2:482). The most conspicuous thing about this list is the absence from it of the name of Jonathan Swift, an absence which dramatically calls attention to itself; for who had suffered the humiliations of patronage more than Swift himself?

A few months later in "A Panegyric on the Reverend Dean Swift" the absence is made good. The purported author addresses Swift:

> But hark'ee, is it truly so,
> (And you of all Mankind should know)

Press, 1975], 1:552 [items P.36, P.37]). This, says Foxon, suggests that the attribution to Arbuckle may be correct. I am indebted for this information to a paper Aubrey Williams wrote for the Modern Language Association meeting in December 1978. Williams supports the Arbuckle authorship, largely, I think, because he finds the poem so repulsive that he hates to think Swift might have written it. I have no expertise in these matters of attribution. I think Swift was thoroughly capable of writing such a poem, and until stronger negative evidence is forthcoming I shall accept the attributions of Ball and Harold Williams as authoritative. The letters to Bathhurst and Gay are in *Correspondence,* ed. Williams, 3:410–11, 418.

> That Men of *Wit* can be no more
> Than *Pimps* to Wickedness in *Pow'r?* (2:493)

And again, probing the sore more deeply:

> No Wonder you should think it *little*
> To *lick a Rascal Statesman's Spittle,*
> Who have, to shew your great Devotion,
> Oft' swallow'd down a stronger Potion,
> A Composition more absurd,
> *Bob's Spittle* mix'd with *Harry*'s T[urd]. (2:495)

(Bob is Robert Harley, Lord Oxford; Harry is Henry St. John, Viscount Bolingbroke.)

Swift's education in the realities of social and political power must have been excruciatingly painful for one of his temperament. His endlessly reiterated boasts about his independence of those in high station are flatly contradicted by his prolonged and humiliating struggle for preferment in the Church. For all the expressions of gratitude (doubtless sincere) to Sir William Temple, for all the show of camaraderie with Oxford and Bolingbroke, Swift must always have been aware that the dependency situation carried with it the implication that he was using his talents as a whore uses her charms. Some of the pain of this awareness comes through in the *Journal to Stella* and the correspondence, but much of it must have been repressed. Through the mouth of the "enemy," the "Scrubb libeller" who writes "A Panegyric on the Reverend Dean Swift," an element of what was repressed finds dreadful voice. The poem asserts that the moral armature holding together Swift's life is rotten throughout. Why does he write satire? the poem asks. To gratify his pride. He is accused of not believing in God; of having achieved his deanship by crooked means and of being resentful that he was not made a bishop; of providing a corrupt model for others in matters of language and sentiments; of leading the mob which once he despised; of sharing Gulliver's misanthropic view at the end of his travels that "Humankind are all

Yahoos." Finally, an ambiguously comic note: Swift is accused of wanting to be a horse.[5]

Of all Swift's notorious self-lacerations, I know of none worse than this poem. Our own century has a peculiar talent for self-punishment, and for me Swift's "Panegyric" has a uniquely twentieth-century character, an R. D. Laingian character. It reminds me of Martha Quest's willed plunge into madness in order to explore her own being in Doris Lessing's *Four-Gated City*. In that dreadful episode Martha hears herself uttering anti-Semitic statements, sounding like Goebbels; she discovers herself saying things, feeling things, that are the complete opposite of what the sane and rational Martha believes. "I've been turned inside out like a glove," she says. "I've been like the negative of a photograph. Or a mirror image. I've seen the underneath of myself. Which isn't me—anymore than my surface is me." The search for the self takes people like Swift and Martha Quest (and surely Doris Lessing) into dark and normally forbidden places. It must have been a strong compulsion that would have prompted Jonathan Swift to present that inside-out version of himself for public inspection. The protective conventions of irony here fail utterly.[6]

One or two of Swift's Imitations of Horace deal with some of this same explosive material—in particular, the matter of patronage—but as Nora Jaffe suggests in her recent book, *The Poet Swift,* the imitative form may have curbed his chaotic feelings. The imitation of part of the seventh *Epistle* of the first book of Horace contains an amusing presentation of Swift as a reluctant recipient of Lord Oxford's patronage, ruined by the deanship which Oxford has thrust upon him. The Imitation is by no means symmetrical with Horace's original, in which Horace defends his refusal to come down to Rome to attend on his patron Maecenas. Although grateful for all Maecenas has

5. Properly read, the last lines of the "Panegyric" constitute an interesting gloss by Swift on what have become major critical issues in the reading of *Gulliver's Travels,* book 4.

6. Doris Lessing, *Four-Gated City* (London: Pantheon, 1972), 554–69.

done for him, he insists on maintaining his independence. If necessary, says Horace, he will cheerfully return all Maecenas' gifts. The poem ends with a carefully elaborated tale illustrating the case of a simple man, Volteius Mena, who has been plucked out of a lowly but independent life by an unsolicited patron, Philippus, and thrust into a richer, more complex mode of living. Prosperity sours immediately; Mena finds himself miserable and begs his patron to return him to the old simple way of life.

   Swift imitates only this last part of Horace's poem. He casts himself, not as Horace (except insofar as he is writing the poem) but as Mena; Lord Oxford he puts in the role of the patron Philippus. Whereas the thrust of Horace's poem is toward the poet's statement of independence from the obligations of patronage, Swift's Imitation constitutes a good-humored complaint that he has been victimized by the malicious generosity of his patron, Oxford. Having been appointed to the deanship in Dublin,

> Poor S[wift] departs, and, what is worse,
> With borrow'd Money in his Purse.

A litany of his deanly woes follows:

> Suppose him gone through all Vexations,
> Patents, Instalments, Abjurations,
> First-Fruits and Tenths, and Chapter-Treats,
> Dues, Payments, Fees, Demands and Cheats,
> (The wicked Laity's contriving,
> To hinder Clergymen from thriving);
> Now all the Doctor's Money's spent, . . . (1:173–74)

A thousand pounds in debt, the Dean posts back to Lord Oxford and makes the same plea that Horace's Mena had made: *vitae me redde priori.* No statement of the poet's independence here; instead an amusing rewriting of the history of Swift's agonized search for preferment and an oblique suggestion that his money losses attendant on the deanship be made up.

   Early in the Imitation we are given a characterization of Swift

ostensibly by Erasmus Lewis, Oxford's secretary. Lewis por-
trays a bluff, man-of-the-world Swift, known for avoiding his
fellow clergymen, for going where he wants, saying what he
pleases; a person of wit and strong opinions, indebted to nobody, very much his own man. By the end of the poem this
same Swift is very much Oxford's man, begging to be returned
to his former independent state. Historically, we know this is
nonsense, the last thing Dean Swift would have wanted. That is,
the "Swift" presented in the poem does not represent the sentiments of the historical Swift any more than the account in the
poem of Swift's first meeting with Robert Harley represents
historical truth. For that particular historical truth, or a closer
approximation thereof, we go to the *Journal to Stella,* where
Swift's presentation of himself has a more privileged status.
There is historical truth, however, to Swift's claim to £1000
reimbursement from the government, and we know his re-
luctance to press that claim. The Horatian model, calling for
Swift to present himself in the poem as eager to get out from
under the burden of patronage, unquestionably does represent in
some sense Swift's own feelings; but at the same time the presentation of self is designed to tease money from my Lord Trea-
surer. Even Horace is caught in this dilemma: if he keeps his
independence and his gifts from Maecenas, he is that much more
indebted to his patron. Swift wants his independence (but not at
the price of the deanship), and he wants the £1000 the deanship
has cost him. Out of conflict of this kind was born the ugly truth
to which, nearly twenty years later, the "enemy" points when
in his guise Swift writes "A Panegyric on the Reverend Dean
Swift."

Of all Swift's poems the most celebrated is the "Verses on the
Death of Dr. Swift," a bravura exercise in the presentation-of-
self mode. Writing to John Gay in December 1731, Swift very
amusingly conjures his poem nearly out of existence:

> I have been severall months writing near five hundred lines on
> a pleasant Subject, onely to tell what my friends and enemyes

will say on me after I am dead. I Shall finish it soon, for I add
two lines every week, and blott out four, and alter eight.[7]

There is universal agreement that the first 300 lines of the poem
constitute a remarkable tour de force as Swift, writing in the first
person, tests the claim of La Rochefoucauld's maxim: "In the
Adversity of our best Friends, we find something that doth not
displease us":

> Vain human Kind! Fantastick Race!
> Thy various Follies, who can trace?
> Self-love, Ambition, Envy, Pride,
> Their Empire in our Hearts divide.

Who is the best example? Swift himself:

> In Pope, I cannot read a Line,
> But with a Sigh, I wish it mine:
> When he can in one Couplet fix
> More sense than I can do in Six:
> It gives me such a jealous Fit,
> I cry, Pox take him, and his Wit.
> Why must I be outdone by Gay,
> In my own hum'rous biting Way?
>
> Arbuthnot is no more my Friend,
> Who dares to Irony pretend;
> Which I was born to introduce,
> Refin'd it first, and shew'd its Use . . .
>
> To all my Foes, dear Fortune, send
> Thy Gifts, but never to my Friend. (2:555)

From this disarming confessional mode we move out of the first
person into a buzz of anonymous comment on the Dean's fading
abilities, his approaching demise:

7. Swift, *Correspondence,* 3:506. For a comprehensive and balanced study of the
poem see Arthur H. Scouten and Robert D. Hume, "Pope and Swift: Text and
Interpretation of Swift's Verses on His Death," *Philological Quarterly* 52 (1973):
205–31.

> For Poetry, he's past his Prime,
> He takes an Hour to find a Rhime:
> His Fire is out, his Wit decay'd,
> His Fancy sunk, his Muse a Jade. . . .
> I wish he may hold out till Spring. (2:556–57)

Then after the fatal day has come, a chorus of heartless, vapid chatter:

> My female Friends, whose tender Hearts
> Have better learn'd to act their Parts,
> Receive the News in *doeful Dumps,*
> "The Dean is dead, *(And what is Trumps?)*
> "Then Lord have Mercy on his Soul.
> "(Ladies I'll venture for the *Vole.*)
> "Six Deans they say must bear the Pall.
> "(I wish I knew what *King* to call.) (2:562)

Nobody does this kind of thing better than Swift. He writes of his slide into senility in lines sparkling with wit, the performance belying the profession, the self-deprecation carrying its own denial. Social commentary critical of the Dean is so obviously biased and self-serving that it redounds to the Dean's credit. Not even Horace presents himself more deftly to his own advantage.

Even of the first two-thirds of the "Verses on the Death," however, this is not the whole story. Beginning at line 168 with a reference to the Dean's role as Drapier, a subtextual commentary on the poem in the form of explanatory footnotes obtrudes itself. The notes are written in the third person in the hectoring, obsessive prose of Swift's late years, the stridency from the bottom of the page clashing unpleasantly with the beautifully controlled tone of the verse. Indeed, verse and prose might have been written by different people; they were certainly written at different times, in very different moods, under different stars.

The last third of the poem, the controversial "character" of Dean Swift by an allegedly impartial speaker, represents still another Swift—not, I think, a Swift drawn in exaggerated colors for ironic purposes, as some critics claim, but Swift as (particularly in his old age) he conceived of himself, as he wanted himself to be. Once again, he mythologizes himself into the traditional figure of the Satirist. This time, however, despite the stylistic intimations of the first part of the poem, his ironic fences are down and the tutelary figure of Horace is inadequate to contain the image; instead, Swift makes himself into a more heroic, more moralistic, more Juvenalian figure. As he knew, all major satirists—Horace, Persius, Juvenal, Régnier, Boileau, Pope—all had made extravagant claims for the rectitude of their motives and the sanative effect of their practice. Like Swift's, their verse was

> with a moral View design'd
> To cure the Vices of Mankind.

Each had protested that

> Malice never was his Aim;
> He lash'd the Vice but spar'd the Name. (2:571)[8]

Similarly, the convention calls for satirists who justify their calling to present themselves in highly flattering lights. Thus Swift had eminent precedent. But the sense of measure and of scale which Boileau maintains, for example, and Pope in the "Epistle to Dr. Arbuthnot," a sense which has presided over the first part of the "Verses on the Death," deserts Swift at the end. Here are some lines from the character of Dean Swift as presented by a supposedly impartial speaker to a group assembled at the Rose Tavern:

> "He never courted Men in Station,
> "*Nor Persons had in Admiration;*
> "Of no Man's Greatness was afraid,
> "Because he sought for no Man's Aid.
> "Though trusted long in great Affairs,
> "He gave himself no haughty Airs:

---

8. On the Juvenalian Swift, see Ronald Paulson's discussion in *The Fictions of Satire* (Baltimore: Johns Hopkins University Press, 1967), 196–210.

> "Withought regarding private Ends,
> "Spent all his Credit for his Friends:
> "And only chose the Wise and Good. (2:565–66)

Or again:

> "... Power was never in his Thought;
> "And, Wealth he valu'd not a Groat. (2:567)

Or again:

> "By Innocence and Resolution,
> "He bore continual Persecution. . . .
> "But Heav'n his Innocence defends,
> "The grateful People stand his Friends. (2:569–70)

In passages like these, Swift's vision of himself as persecuted innocent, as heroic defender of righteousness, uncontaminated by the folly of the world, burgeons out of control. The intemperance of the footnotes spills over into the verse; under the strain of emotion even the syntax breaks down as the allegedly impartial speaker inadvertently identifies himself with Swift. This happens in a passage praising the efforts of Lords Oxford and Bolingbroke to save their sinking country. With the Queen's death, however, all was lost. The speaker in this part of the poem, characterized as "One quite indifferent in the cause," puts the matter thus:

> "And, oh! how short are human Schemes!
> Here ended all our golden Dreams. . . .
> Too soon that precious Life was ended,
> On which alone, our Weal depended." (2:567–68)

In this poignant moment the distance between the fictive "impartial" speaker and Jonathan Swift collapses: the third person pronoun *his* suddenly becomes the first person *our* as the speaker, no longer even in formal terms impartial, injects himself into the drama. He and Jonathan Swift become indistinguishable. The mythologizing in this latter part of the poem has gone well beyond belief.

Alexander Pope's judgment of the poem was just. When he
and Dr. William King saw the "Verses on the Death" into print,
they dropped the footnotes and almost the entire "impartial"
character on the grounds that it made Swift look vain and was in
fact in a number of places untrue. In its place they substituted a
more balanced, more dialectically Horatian presentation of self,
from an earlier poem, "The Life and Character of Dr. Swift."
This must have seemed to Swift a violation of an intensely personal kind. His most "sincere" presentation of self, the one in
which he as a performer was, in Goffman's language, "most
fully taken in by his own act," had been killed off by Pope, and
without his permission. No wonder he contravened Pope's edi-
torial decision immediately by rushing into print his own
"truer" version of himself, footnotes and all. If truth about the
self—or truth about one's feelings about the self—is the issue (as
I think it was for Swift), then he was doubtless justified; but
from an aesthetic point of view Pope, as I say, was right. The
"impartial" character of the "Verses on the Death" founders in
its own sincerity, its own Romantic quality, to pick up a hint
from Ronald Paulson. It is redeemed only by these last splendid
half-dozen lines:

> "He gave the little Wealth he had,
> To build a House for Fools and Mad:
> And shew'd by one satyric Touch,
> No Nation wanted it so much:
> That Kingdom he hath left his Debtor,
> I wish it soon may have a Better." (2:572)

As Edward Said says, " 'the Verses [on the Death]' deliver Swift
to history at the poem's end."[9]

This discussion has omitted many poems bearing on our
theme: "Cadenus and Vanessa," the charming "Apology to the
Lady Carteret," many others in which Swift plays the game of
presenting himself in verse to an audience. Indeed, the whole

9. Edward Said, "Swift's Tory Anarchy," *Eighteenth-Century Studies* 3 (1969–
70): 66.

enterprise may be thought of as a game, a game of charades in which each persona, each mask adopted by the maker, approximates more or less closely to what we think of as the real Swift. And who is the real Swift? It is hopeless, of course, to inquire. Nevertheless, just as each of us has at the back of his or her head a concept of Truth or Justice adequate, if not to allow us to say what Truth or Justice definitively is, at least to say what they are not, so each of us has a concept of the real Jonathan Swift vivid enough to enable us to discriminate among the many selves he presents. We must take those selves seriously, all of them. As Goffman says, "Words are mere and shouldn't be worth anything at all, but, in fact, every statement, in one way or another, is a performative utterance."[10] All Swift's selves are true; but some, of course, are much truer than others.

10. Goffman, *Strategic Interaction* (New York: Ballantine Books, 1972), 171.

9 Conclusion

The conclusion reached in the last chapter—all Swift's selves are real, but some are more real than others—is unlikely to seem entirely satisfactory, despite any marginal support it might garner from the allusion to Orwell's famous play with the word *equality* in *Animal Farm.* But Orwell's paradox had satiric bite and in its literal absurdity an element of comedy. Nothing of this is present in the comment on the reality of Swift's selves—only a flat statement of logical contradiction. Like most paradoxes put forward as the solution to a complex problem, it looks like an evasion, the kind of evasion that has been resorted to at other analytic cruxes in this book, as when, for example, it was said that the "I" of "Skunk Hour" both is and is not to be identified with Robert Lowell. So with various contradictory comments bearing on the relation of persona to self. As should be clear by now, however, when the subject of the self is in question, the law of contradiction does not hold.

Poets have long known this. "I am not I; pity the tale of me," writes Sidney in Sonnet 45. Coleridge characterizes Shakespeare as one who becomes all things, yet forever remains the same. Keats writes of the poetical Character ("of which, if I am anything, I am a Member") that "it has no self—it is every thing and nothing—It has no character. . . . A Poet. . . has no Identity."[1] Interpreters of poetry in our formally self-conscious age found the paradoxes associated with the poet's use of the first person singular pronoun bafflingly difficult to deal with: when, if ever, are the poetic "I" and the empirical "I" truly one? Shortly after World War II, following on the usage of Pound and Yeats and Carl Jung, they introduced the term *persona* into critical discourse as a way of coming to terms with the paradoxes. As we saw in chapter five, similar paradoxes are generated when, outside poetry, social scientists like William James and Erving Goffman attempt to understand the nature of the self. The term *persona* has proved useful, even indispensable, in this enterprise too. But the paradoxes remain, as in Dahrendorf's analysis of homo sociologicus: man as at once an autonomous moral agent and an alienated being. However, as again we saw in chapter five, the assertion of paradox as the solution of difficult problems whether in atomic physics, in what Vincent Buckley calls the I-grammar of poetry, or in the analysis of self need not be thought of as intellectual evasion. That is, to say that the poetic "I" and the empirical "I" are, and are not, truly one is not an irresponsible play with language. In these matters the angle of vision employed governs entirely; it is the humanist's equivalent of the scientist's microscope. Approached under the aspect of Niels Bohr's theory of complementarity, such paradoxes afford their own kind of light.

Yeats might well have been telling us this in his great poem "Among School Children," which was written at about the time Niels Bohr was developing his theory. The poem, as Robert Langbaum says, has at its center the question of identity: where among all the metamorphoses of life, from infancy to old age, is the real person?[2] The answer, in the "gorgeous questions" with which the poem ends, is paradoxical; it fits perfectly into the complementary mode of thinking of William James and Niels Bohr:

1. Keats, *Letters,* ed. Rollins, 1:387.
2. Langbaum, *Mysteries of Identity,* 223–24.

O chestnut-tree, great rooted blossomer,
Are you the leaf, the blossom or the bole?
O body swayed to music, O brightening glance,
How can we know the dancer from the dance?

Index